GEORGE HALDEN EARLE

A Concert Unto Himself

Cyril F. Poole

GEORGE HALDEN EARLE
A Concert Unto Himself
Cyril F. Poole

CREATIVE PUBLISHERS
St. John's, Newfoundland
2001

Le Conseil des Arts | The Canada Council
du Canada | for the Arts

We acknowledge the support of The Canada Council for the Arts for our
publishing program.

We acknowledge the financial support of the Government of Canada
through the Book Publishing Industry Development Program (BPIDP)
for our publishing activities.

Cover: Canon George Earle in the role of Jethro Noddy,
in the CBC Production of Ted Russell's
Tales of Pidgeon Inlet.
Photo by Don Lane

∞ Printed on acid-free paper

Published by
CREATIVE BOOK PUBLISHING
a division of 10366 Newfoundland Limited
a Robinson-Blackmore Printing & Publishing associated company
P.O. Box 8660, St. John's, Newfoundland A1B 3T7

Printed in Canada by:
ROBINSON-BLACKMORE PRINTING & PUBLISHING

National Library of Canada Cataloguing in Publication Data

Poole, Cyril F.,
George Halden Earle : a concert unto himself

ISBN 1-894294-37-8

1. Earle, George Halden, 1914-2000 2. Anglican Church of Canada —
Clergy — Biography. 3. Clergy—Newfoundland — St. John's —
Biography. 4. Queen's College (St. John's, Nfld.)—Biography. I. Title.

BX5620.E27P66 2001   283'.092   C2001-901478-3

To my parents
Dorman and Blanche

CONTENTS

PREFACE

While this biography covers the highlights of Canon Earle's distinguished career as an Anglican priest, including his twenty-two years as Provost of Queen's College, its focus is his rich outport heritage and his humorous celebration of it in prose and verse and in upwards of a thousand after-dinner speeches. In the tribute he once paid his fun-loving grandfather, George Earle was "a concert unto himself." While making tens of thousands of Newfoundlanders laugh at ourselves he heightened our pride of place and people.

My chief sources of information were Earle's own writing, much of it unpublished; lengthy diaries he kept in 1938 as Chaplain to Bishop Abraham on a coastal tour of Newfoundland and during the war years in England; a dozen interviews with him in 1998 and 1999; abd a close friendship. I am deeply indebted to his wife Elna for ferreting out rich material about which he had not told me, and for supplementing documentary information. For interviews I also thank the Earle children, Christine, Alison and Peter; George's sisters June (Butler) and Mabel (Kirby), and his brothers Frederick and Charles; his longtime friend Otto Tucker, the Right Reverend S.S. Payne and John Gullage.

I am also grateful to Harry Cuff Publications for permission to quote from Earle's *Old Foolishness or Folklore?*, to Carrie Scammell for permission to quote verses from her late husband's moving war poem "These Shall Not Return," and to Don Lane for use of the cover photograph. Finally, I thank Dr. Harry Steele for facilitating publication, Catherine Colwell for meticulous secretarial work and my son Stephen for unsparing criticism of the manuscript.

—Cyril F. Poole
Sackville, N.B.
June, 2001

The Earles of Change Islands

George Halden Earle was born in Change Islands, Notre Dame Bay on March 21, 1914. At the age of fourteen he moved to Fogo with his family. But it was Change Islands that he would always regard as home. For George the community remained not just his birthplace but the Arcadia of his memories and values. The "indelible recording" it made on his psyche was not in his case a romanticized memory of a happy childhood; it was as cerebral as it was emotional. In virtually all of his after-dinner speeches and even in some of·his sermons he drew on his Change Islands boyhood for values, language and illustrations. Although he sometimes went out of his way to say that Change Islands was a typical outport, in fact he regarded it as a superior one. "If a community were too tiny," he wrote in the *Book of Newfoundland* (bk IV), "it would have an inferiority complex; if an old centre of merchants and skippers it would have a superiority complex. Change Islands came in between and was her natural self without airs of superiority or feelings of inferiority and laughed at herself instead of despising others and in the process built a strong community with all kinds of characters to give it flavour."

Change Islands, George proudly told a 1979 Memorial University convocation in which he received an honorary doctorate, "was a school in itself, knowing intimately a cross-section of humanity, which I think is infinitely preferable to knowing a large number superficially." The question of whether Change Islands was the superior community George clearly thought it to be comes up again. For now it is enough to say that it was the same community in which a fifteen-year-old boy wrote "The Squid-Jiggin' Ground" immortalizing such characters as skipper John Chaffey and poor uncle Billy, old Billy Cave and a red-headed Tory. Scammell's writing, like Earle's, is infused with affection and gratitude for the community that nurtured him. "I suppose," Scammell wrote in later years, "all Newfoundland outports have their 'characters,' but we on Change Islands were especially blessed in this regard. We all took a proprietary interest in them. There was time to enjoy and cultivate wit, humour, and the lighter side of life." Change Islands people had a "delightful sense of humour, real humour of character and situation, that bubbled in the darkest days." Few communities in Newfoundland have been celebrated by native sons and daughters with such joy and affection.

The Change Islands in which George Earle was born in 1914 was one of the most prosperous and stimulating fishing communities in Newfoundland. Much younger than some nearby communities such as Fogo, Joe Batt's Arm and Twillingate, it had a population of only 316 in 1845. In the next forty years, however, it experienced the rapid growth of a boom town, the population tripling to over 900 by the 1890s. In the years between World War I and the Depression, when Earle and Scammell were boys, the inshore cod, herring and salmon fishery flourished, while each spring saw around fifty Change Islands schooners set sail for the Labrador fishery. And by the 1870s the community, ideally situated, had become a focal point of the seal fishery.

The economic prosperity and the large population brought immediate cultural and social benefits. Change

Islands could attract more than its share of qualified teachers, better educated and more cosmopolitan clergymen, customs officers and a medical doctor. But unlike Fogo, George once quipped, the "fine citizens of Change Islands didn't need a policeman." And "we were not ingrown because there was lots of new blood coming into the community." Adding to the sense of self-confidence and optimism were the facts that Change Islands was a port of call for coastal boats, foreign ships bringing salt and other supplies and loading salt cod for Europe and South America, and was the centre of two of the largest mercantile firms in the area. One of the first four Notre Dame Bay communities to form a branch of the Fishermen's Protective Union, Change Islands was chosen the next year, 1909, as the site of the Supreme Council meeting of the Union. "We were large and prosperous enough," George would have us believe, "to be self-confident, but not, like Fogo, big enough to be cocky."

The course the Earles took from Dartmouth, Devon to St. John's and north to Notre Dame Bay diverged sharply from the route taken by most Newfoundland settlers and by virtually all of the people in Notre Dame Bay. Their first Newfoundland ancestor, Henry, was born in Dartmouth in 1809 and came to St. John's sometime between 1835 and 1840, not as a fisherman or in a business connected with the fishery but as tailor to the Military Garrison in St. John's. When the Garrison closed in 1870 he established a successful tailoring business near the waterfront. Meanwhile Henry and his wife Catherine Paige, who was seven years his junior, had reared a large family of sons and daughters, some of whom remained on the Avalon Peninsula, others going on to good jobs in Canada. Catherine died in 1868, Henry in 1883. Both were buried in the Church of England cemetery, Forest Road, St. John's.

Henry J., born in 1840, the eldest son of Henry and Catherine, went north to Twillingate, once again not into the fishery but as a music teacher. A strong musical strain ran through the Earle family from the first Henry to children and great-great grandchildren. The third son of Henry and Catherine, Samuel, became longtime organist at the Anglican Cathedral in Charlottetown, Prince Edward Island, a grandson, Frederick Ralph, George's father, was a church organist for twenty-seven years, a great-granddaughter, June, served as organist in the Fogo church until she married and left home, while the strain was marked in several of George's other siblings.

Although a northerly and isolated community, Twillingate already boasted the beginnings of a musical tradition that would soon foster the talents of the Stirling sisters, including Georgina, "The Nightingale of the North," the Berteau and Tobin children, two of whom would go on to Mount St. Vincent College in Halifax for further study, and the talented young daughter of the Rev. Robert Temple, whose mother was the church organist and music teacher. The schools and churches, especially St. Peter's Church of England, gave sustained support to both music and drama. (A brief account of the musical tradition of Twillingate is given by Amy Louise Peyton in her biography of Georgina Stirling.) It was to this "Capital of the North" that the young Henry J. Earle sailed for a career as a music teacher.

There are accidents in human affairs that decree where a child will be born and, therefore, the kind of person he will become. A chance friendship radically altered the course of Henry J.'s life and determined that George would be born a Change Islander. After teacher Henry became a close friend of John Owen, a bookkeeper in the Poole, Dorset firm of John Slade & Co., he too joined the firm. Soon thereafter the two friends purchased the business, operating under the name Owen and Earle. Henry moved to Fogo to manage the large branches there and in Change Islands. The firm became Henry J. Earle & Sons after Henry became the sole owner in 1897. Henry died in 1933 at the ripe age of ninety-three, but the business was carried on by his family as Earle Sons & Co. until about 1970.

Meanwhile at Henry's invitation in the early 1880s his youngest brother Frederick Charles, born in 1855, became manager of the firm's Change Islands branch. He was to become the patriarch of the Change Islands Earles and George's grandfather. The decision to move to an isolated, northern community must have been a difficult one. Coming from a tailor's family in St. John's, he had no knowledge of the fisheries that were the heart of the business. Moreover he had been for some time nicely settled in Toronto. To complicate the decision, he had married a Toronto woman for whom Change Islands loomed at the very edge of the world, her style of life ill-suited to a Newfoundland fishing village. Born in Rochester, New York, Louisa Julia, daughter of Joshua and Mary Halden, was twenty-six when she married twenty-seven year old Charles in 1882. How Charles, a young immigrant from a remote, insular country gained an entree to Julia's social circle is no doubt partly explained by the fact that they both worked at T. Eaton's. Perhaps it was his sense of humour and love of music and drama that attracted her — for all of which he was to be celebrated in the Change Islands and Fogo areas of Notre Dame Bay.

Julia's interests included skiing and membership in a Toronto pony club, where one of her friends was a niece (or perhaps a sister) of Mrs. Timothy Eaton. While Eaton's was not then the household name it was soon to become, Timothy had opened a Toronto store a decade earlier and the first Eaton's Catalogue would appear within two years

Grandmother and Grandfather Earle, c.1880.

of Julia's marriage. That Julia was more than a casual acquaintance of the Eaton family is shown by the fact that they gave her a splendid silver tea set as a wedding gift. Clearly her style of life was in sharp contrast with that of a Newfoundland outport woman in the 1880s. A studio photograph taken at the time of her marriage shows a composed and pensive expression, her strong chin and firm mouth suggesting strength and self-assurance. A triple necklace and a dangling, multiple waist-chain with pendant enhance the picture of a beautiful and elegant woman.

Among the questions Julia asked her husband before they left for Change Islands was whether there were any ponies and ski slopes in the community. Truthfully, but without elaboration, Frederick Charles assured her that many families owned a pony and that there were lots of hills. And thus it was that she arrived in Change Islands complete with riding tack. It was first used nearly four decades later when her grandson Fred "discovered it in the barn and darn well made good use of it." Although there is no evidence that the young bride felt sorry for herself, the image of her walking down the gangplank to the coastal wharf "in all her finery," as one family member put it, evokes a certain amount of pity. She was met by a curious, silent group of liveyers lined up for inspection with the mien of an honour guard. It was after all not every day that a foreigner came to live among them, the wife withal of the new manager of Earle's who himself was from the capital by way of Toronto.

Her granddaughter Julia (June) recalls her grandmother's telling her how she underwent the same critical inspection when she first went to church. Witnessing on leaving the church a "guard of honour, especially of women," assembled to size up her clothes, she resolved, as she told her husband, that "Henceforth I'll dress like the women here." While this resolve was a symbol of her admirable wish to become one of the Islanders, it was her fate, not surprisingly, always to be known as the Mrs. Earle. She and Frederick Charles certainly brought to Change Islands some of the new blood to which George was to attribute much of the vitality and *joie de vivre* of the community.

The couple remained in Change Islands for the rest of their lives, Frederick Charles as manager of the Earle business and village character and entertainer, Julia as mother of a large family and community leader, both as much loved parents and grandparents. Of their nine children only six survived into adulthood. The first child, George Halden, died in 1885 under two years old, Frederick Charles when only ten days old and Gertrude Olive in 1890 just past her second birthday as the result of a scalding accident. "Imagine 1885 for Grandpa and Grandma," George was to write on a page of the family tree, " — the loss of

their first two sons within six months of each other."
George's father, Frederick Ralph, born August 15, 1886,
was the oldest surviving child. His grandmother died in
1924 at age sixty-eight, his grandfather at age seventy-five
in 1930 when George was sixteen.

George's father, Fred, who from his boyhood han-
kered after the outdoor life afforded by outports, chose to
remain in Change Islands. On finishing grade six, i.e. Book
Six of the *Royal Readers,* he left school at the age of thirteen
or fourteen and, with a flair for mathematics, became an
apprenticed bookkeeper in the Earle business. He worked
as bookkeeper in Change Islands and, after 1928, in Fogo
until the business wound up operations in about 1970. Like
his father, Fred was an employee of the company, never
having owned shares. His peak salary as a bookkeeper was
$1500, but this was reduced to $1200 during the Depression.

One of Fred's classmates was Bertha Oake, a bright girl
three months his junior, who also finished school in grade
six. Also of a large family, she was a daughter of Annie
(Hynes) and Josiah Oake, an enterprising inshore fisherman remembered by his grandson George as a "discipli-
narian and a man of rigid religious proscriptions." Married
to Fred in her mid-twenties, Bertha was to bear eleven
children, the first of whom died at birth. The other ten, of
whom George was the second, were born between 1912
and 1928, when Bertha was forty-two. In order of birth
George's siblings were Frederick Leslie, Julia Mary (June),
Bertha Jean, Mabel Elizabeth, Harry Oake, Edna Carrie,
Charles Weston, Ethel Margaret and Gertrude Vivian.

Under the best of circumstances housekeeping and the
bearing and bringing up of a family is surely one of the
most demanding of vocations. When, without any of our
modern household aids, Bertha was bringing up her large
family the task, in time alone, must have been nothing

Grandmother and Grandfather Oake, 1934.

short of daunting, a kind of voluntary servitude. In addition to the routine work, the four seasons saw Bertha bottling and canning the prodigious amounts of fish, wild meat and berries her husband brought home from ocean and woodland. On her, as on most mothers, also fell much of the day-to-day planning for school and such activities as music lessons. With all this, Bertha was a leader in church and Sunday school. When June, her third child, was only an infant her mother came down with a prolonged illness and, diagnosed with tuberculosis, was sent to a hospital in St. John's. Under the stress of having to leave three young children in the care of their father and grandmother Julia, she wrote her husband a series of letters pleading for release from the hospital. Kept in the hospital, she pleaded, she would die anyway. And so, after some weeks she was allowed to return home, apparently in satisfactory health, and in the next eleven years bore seven more children. (It appeared later, when no scar or lesion showed up on her lung, that tuberculosis had been an incorrect diagnosis.)

The simple tribute, "A Vocation Fulfilled," George paid his mother on her death in February 1959 reads in part:

> Ten sons and daughters on her funeral day
> Recall, with thanks the mother who held sway
> And ruled with loving kindness those she bore
> And ever slept with open ear and door.
>
> Inspecting work for day and Sunday school,
> Or keeping fevered patients gently cool,
> Or giving each a happy birthday treat,
> Or mustard baths for wet and frozen feet.
>
> So morally correct, yet not a prude;
> So humorous, yet scorning what was crude;
> So fond of 'cruising,' yet without neglect
> Of any child she felt she should protect.
>
> This estimate has not been half its plan
> But quietly we love her life to scan
> And pray in union with the Christ above
> That she enjoy his pardon, peace and love.

The tribute mentions Bertha's interest in 'cruising.' In 1956, when she was seventy, she took a cruise to England to visit George in his Choppington parish. Despite having a white-collar father, George and his siblings were often 'enslaved' in the hateful chores from which few outport children escaped. For their father, driven by necessity, supplemented his bookkeeper's income from a variety of outport sources — a vegetable garden, hens, a small fox farm, pigs and goats and by fishing and hunting. Produce over and above family needs was sold. A "real outporter," as George termed him, when he was not driven to the woods and fishing grounds by necessity he was pulled by instinct. In the summers, his eldest son Fred recalls, "he always fished from daylight to breakfast, first from cod traps and after the capelin landed from trawls." Quickly replacing guernsey and oilskins with the obligatory shirt and tie, he would check himself in at the office that was his prison.

Depending on the season, the kitchen was a production line of canned and bottled cod, mussels, pickled herring, rabbit and turrs, vegetables and berries. Rare but profitable bakeapples were scrounged and canned when spring frost hadn't killed them off. In 1927, when George was thirteen, thirty-three cases of bakeapples or almost fifteen hundred pounds were sold in New York. This feverish activity had to be carried on while barnyard animals called for attention. When in 1928 George's father was appointed head bookkeeper in Fogo the firm's large boat, still remembered as Noah's Ark, pulled out from the Change Islands wharf loaded not only with the normal household goods and nine children, but cluttered with several goats, a grunting pig, a pony and fifty chattering hens.

As the youngsters reached draft age they were conscripted into distasteful outport chores. Unlike his eldest

George and sister June, Change Islands.

brother Fred and his father, George had no great taste for
hauling nets and lobster pots, and none at all for weeding
gardens and cleaning chicken coops. And he certainly
didn't need any encouragement to steer clear of the squid-
jiggin' ground. Whenever possible he took refuge in
schoolbooks and homework. In this ruse he was abetted by
his mother. "George can't feed the hens today — he's at his
homework," "George is at his books — don't disturb him
now," "George is studying for exams and can't dig potatoes today." Irritated by the inordinate amount of time
George spent reading in the outdoor toilet, his father one
day dubbed it "The Study," the designation by which it

was known thereafter. While George's siblings, like their mother, regarded him as a studious boy, he himself always contended that it was never love of learning that kept his nose into books, but a strong aversion to the alternative of domestic drudgery. Whatever his motive, he bordered on being what Art Scammell's characters would call a useless article.

While George may not have had Tom Sawyer's "magnificent inspiration" for getting his friends to whitewash fences, he did hit upon a scheme to get boys to perform some of his most distasteful chores. Noticing one summer that boys in the first stirrings of puberty were hanging around his home in hope of courting one of his good looking sisters, he encouraged the visits, even now and then arranging a glimpse of the girls. With judgment impaired by pubescent love, the boys unwittingly found themselves weeding carrots and turnips, watering the cow and pony or shovelling out the barn. While, unlike Tom Sawyer, George didn't make any money off the scheme he certainly saved himself a lot of drudgery.

Notwithstanding his application to books and homework, George never ran the risk of becoming a teacher's pet. In fact, as one teacher was to remind him in 1938, he was in school the "little imp" that he remained throughout his life. While he often got other pupils into trouble, his specialty was inflicting torment on his teachers. His sister June (Butler) recalls a frightening altercation between George and a male teacher after her brother was suspected of having a wad of gum secreted in his cheek. With the chewing of gum in the schools of the time being one of the three or four most heinous of crimes, the teacher lost no time in launching the trial. "George, take that gum out of your mouth." The teacher's temper, already up to the occasion, flared higher when the accused replied, "I don't have gum in my mouth," and went on chewing. "What are you chewing, then?" "Frankum, sir." "Well," snapped the angry teacher, "frankum is gum." To this assertion the cheeky pupil replied with a question, "Would you, sir, call hardtack cake?" And, taking advantage of the teacher's momentary silence, gave his own answer, "Well, if hard-tack is not cake, frankum is not gum." Although his case was technically airtight, George received the strapping the judge had settled on before the trial began.

For George, as for many boys of the time, a strapping was a badge of honour. His admiring younger brother Charlie remembers how George and his desk mate used to tally their strappings into their desk top to see who was the winner at the end of the year. George himself recalled how, "We kept one teacher going full-time strapping us. We nearly drove him foolish till we broke his spirit. After that he was alright." Presumably George's behaviour im-proved in the Fogo school, for when he was Provost of Queen's College he noted the fact that the School Board one year awarded him, at a wage of $1.00 a month, the responsible job of lighting school fires. In keeping with a longtime habit, the fact was no doubt noted for a future talk, for attached to it is the quip, "Never scorn a buck and never buck a Board." (That sound maxim does not turn up in any of his written speeches.) While in several articles Canon Earle wrote in detail about his own brief teaching career, he nowhere mentions strappings or other punish-ments. Perhaps he felt that it would be unseemly to associ-ate canons with physical violence, or perhaps he was too smart to let his own pupils earn the badge of honour he himself had won.

Despite his distaste for domestic chores and his strata-gems to escape them, George of course didn't get off scot-free. And in fact although he didn't relish the hard work and discomforts of a fishing boat, he was keen on birding and became a good shot. Nonetheless his recollec-

Indian Islands 1931. L to R: George and Brian Earle (with 'auntsaries'), Len Ludlow (with 'pigeon').

tions of boyhood, more so than his friend Scammell's, highlight fun and games throughout the year and in the summers "swimming or berry-picking or just roaming through the woods or combing the beaches for strange fish or shells" (*Book of Newfoundland*, bk IV, in which Art Scammell also has an article on Change Islands memories). A highlight of summers from the time when George was only eight was the week-long trip "up the bay" with his father and brother Fred. Provisioned for a long stay, the boat carried "all kinds of containers for berries, a canvas tent in case we couldn't find a tilt, guns for birds and a big jar of water in the event of water failure in the brook." Exploring such enchanting places as Hunt's Cove, Squashberry Cove and Dog Bay Islands, all frequented by man-eating animals (the viciousness of which would one day be recounted to children in an English rectory), the adventurers would return home with "red currants, gooseberries and raspberries...shell-birds, pigeons, toggles and occa-

sionally a wild goose or two and some ducks if lucky"
("How We Got Around Then").

The highlight of the summer, especially for young
people in advanced stages of pubescence, was the Garden
Party featuring the sexual rites of "King William was King
George's son." This was sung perhaps fifty times over as a
circle of clasped hands side-hopped around a person in the
centre of the ring singing, "Come choose to the east and
choose to the west/Choose the partner you love best." The
lucky person in the ring, having chosen a partner or, if she
happened not to be there, "another with all your heart,"
the expectant suitor was invited to kneel on the 'scarpet'
and "kiss your partner, kiss her sweet." Whereupon, with
the chosen partner now in the ring, the circle again struck
up "King William." Few outporters would disagree with
George's assessment that "the exciting bit...was the climax
that came with the kiss. That was some good in those
puritan days when kisses were private things and wonderful scarce." George's assessment, however, does not give
due weight to the anguish of those who were never chosen
or of those not chosen by the one that they loved best.

Change Islands boys and men played an unnamed
game apparently unknown elsewhere in Newfoundland.
It was, George recalled, "a cross between English cricket,
American baseball and Newfoundland rounders." The
elements of cricket crept in from the English cricket played
there at the turn of the century. (A splendid photograph of
one cricket team taken around 1903 includes George's
grandfather Earle, his father at seventeen or so, Art Scammell's father Arch, and in top hat the Reverend E. Clench.)
Thus when as a student in England George boasted to the
University coach — and lived to regret it — that he had
played cricket in Newfoundland he was only stretching
the truth as his grandfather had done when he told his

Toronto bride that there were ponies and hills on Change Islands.

Fall was soccer season. For a ball, the boys were usually lucky enough to acquire a pig's bladder, which, toughened up in pickle, would last up to a week. After the Christmas concerts and the twelve days of mummering, winter was generally a long and trying time for youngsters, school for most of them only adding to the gloom. Still, for young children there were snowmen to be made and gleefully toppled into the mud and snow. For older boys there were sleds to be made from scrounged pork-barrel staves, as well as a few lighter sleds of flour-barrel staves for the girls. All in all, however, winter was a long, dull season for most youngsters.

But George was blessed above others. Enjoying with his grandfather Earle a rapport that is not given to most grandchildren to experience, George spent every spare hour at his grandparents' home a few yards across a common field listening to grandfather's celebrated story-telling, ballad singing and mimicry. Those performances he lapped up as if he himself were consciously planning to become a wit and storyteller. To top off his pleasure, grandfather allowed him to smoke in his presence, his reasoning being that if young George was going to smoke he should do it under civilized circumstances rather than behind the barn or under the flake, perhaps in bad company. Meanwhile, in this conspiracy, grandfather and grandson entered into a solemn understanding that, under whatever suspicion George fell at home and however severe the grilling, he would never betray his grandfather. It was a singular loss for the sixteen-year-old grandson when on March 29, 1930 his beloved grandfather lost a prolonged fight with cancer.

When black November cloud shrouded the harbour and in the dead-of-winter after the close of navigation,

George and pet transport.

George and his cronies would hang around the twine lofts, where, in the comfort of a red-hot bogie and pungent Jumbo tobacco smoke, they would listen to net-makers and characters just whiling away the time telling tales of the sea and of ghosts and sleeveens. The Labrador fishery naturally generated many of the hair-raising yarns. The narrow escape of the *Harp* when the useless mate ran her over the Horse Islands shoals in breaking seas; the *Norma Jane* in a northeasterly blizzard running bare-pole before the wind all night, her skipper lashed to the wheel for fifteen hours, and ending up as matchwood under Shag Cliff; and putting away fish in Venison Tickle while being devoured by skitties as big as horse-stingers. Often repeated too were stories of the headless ghost turning up behind the Methodist Church before southerly gales and Skipper Henry Jarge's heroic battle with pirates off Tangier while carrying a load of salt-bulk to Naples. To the boys' added edification and delight, interspersed with these stories were tidbits of information on human anatomy and half-whispered references to scattered cases of adultery and numerous cases of fornication. From these sessions in the twine loft came many of George's wonderful anecdotes and some of his skills as a storyteller.

On winter Sabbaths, when outport communities lay dormant and still, even the twine lofts cold and silent, time lay heavy on the hands of youngsters. Few diversions were possible or permitted. The Earle children, however, were more fortunate than most. Because they were a large, musical family, to whose home streams of neighbours were warmly welcomed, they were able to stage their own concerts and hold "church services." Thus with June, who later became the church organist in Fogo, holding the position of choir director and organist, and George appointed clergyman, they often made the parlour vibrate to such favourites as, "Will your anchor hold?," "Lead kindly Light" and "Tell me the old, old story." George always presided as rector, carrying out his role with Anglican form and solemnity. (Although they sometimes wondered how a stutterer would make out in a real pulpit, the family always assumed that George would become a clergyman, whereas he himself on several occasions said that the idea of entering the ministry was never seriously considered until after his teaching experience in Williamsport in 1933.) When concerts were staged the family were treated to performances by grandfather Earle and by their father, whose specialty was mimicry in dialect. As the Change Islands long winter yielded to spring, indoor entertainment of course gave place to another round of domestic chores and outdoor delights.

For the vicar in England and Provost of Queen's College, family life in Change Islands was recollected in joy.

Writing to his brother Fred on September 19, 1939 from
Silksworth, Durham, where he was doing a curacy before
taking up his studies at the University of Durham, he
reflected that, "It is indeed sad about families, how after a
few happy years together they have to scatter everywhere." The letter is signed, "Your loving brother." The
same note was struck in a letter to his parents after Christmas 1940, "I can well imagine that some of the joy was
taken from your Xmas by our absence. May you always be
reassured and comforted that wherever we go we will
never forget what you have both done for us...You gave us
just enough freedom and social life when growing up to
enable us to reflect in gratitude." In a long letter from
Falstone, England on December 30, 1949, in which George
thanks his parents for generous parcels of salt cod and cans
of bakeapples, rabbit and mussels (giving his wife Elna her
"first taste" of that shellfish), and describes the bounty of
gifts his three-year-old daughter Christine had received at
Christmas, he reflects, "My thoughts at Christmas certainly went back to the early days of my own childhood....If I can give my children as many happy memories
to recall in later life as you gave me I will be extremely
happy." He added that he and his brother Harry, who was
then in England, often talked about the pleasures of home.
Equally glowing recollections of home life were given me
by George's sisters June (Butler) and Mabel (Kirby) and by
his youngest brother Charlie.

Even after making full allowance for the nostalgia with
which age often colours childhood, it is clear that George
was nurtured in a creative, fun-loving community and
family that fostered his deep love of place and his celebrated sense of humour. As he remarked in his Silksworth
letter to his brother Fred, happy memories "stand a chap in
good stead."

College Student and Teacher

George Earle was one of the rare outport pupils of the first half of the century who finished school. Blessed with one of the few families who saw any 'future' in education, he was fortunate to have Ted Russell for a teacher in his last two years in Fogo. It was Russell who, with his parents, encouraged him to attend Memorial University College. The first step was taken when, on Russell's information and recommendation, he attended a College summer school in physics as a Junior Matriculation credit for College entrance. The six-week immersion in physics in the summer of 1931 quickened both his interest in higher education and his awareness of the richer life it could bring. He would now become one of Memorial College's 156 students for a year and perhaps take up a teaching career.

But where would the money come from? In 1931 Newfoundland was in the depth of the Depression, unable to meet its debt payments let alone find money for education. Indeed in the very month, June 1931, when George was writing his grade eleven examinations the government was forced by banks and the Canadian government to take the first drastic measure that would lead in 1934 to the appointment by Britain of a Commission of Government. The plight of government and people was so desperate that, as Earle wrote in 1975 in an article about his Memorial days, "The only way to understand a period like the thirties in Newfoundland is to live through it" (*Book of New-foundland*, bk IV). A measure of Newfoundland's financial crisis in George's freshman year is the fact that the annual government grant to Memorial College was cut from $10,000 to $6,000. The doors of the College were in effect closed to most baymen, only about fifteen of its 156 students that year coming from the entire northeast coast from Lumsden to Cape Bauld (Malcolm MacLeod, *A Bridge Built Halfway*).

As real as the financial problem for outporters was, the psychological barrier created by isolation in small communities, and which to this day keeps many outport students from the more prestigious studies of commerce, engineering and medicine, was an even greater deterrent. Inspired by the fact that his friends of Change Islands days, Art Scammell and his brother Cecil, sons of a fisherman, had broken the barrier and abandoned the squid jiggin' grounds the year the Earles left for Fogo, George managed to scrounge up money for College fees and the $25 per month needed for board and lodging. He became in 1933 the first Fogo student to graduate from a two-year program at Memorial even though Fogo was one of the largest of outports.

In St. John's George stayed at Feild Hall, the residence for the handful of outport boys who could attend Bishop Feild College or another city school, most of them sons of merchants or professional people. His article on Memorial days gives an amusing account of life in residence. The defiance of authority that occasionally was to annoy bishops got him into trouble at Feild Hall. Feild College, modelled on English public schools and run mostly by Englishmen, strictly enforced a battery of irksome regulations in residence. There was, for example, a ten o'clock curfew. While some students, like Mose Morgan, resigned themselves to the restriction, the Fogo lad, in whose home restrictions were understood rather than legislated, regularly flouted it. On two occasions he came within a hairbreadth of being turfed out for sneaking in after ten. Table manners were even subject to strict rules. The boys had to be present for grace at all meals. Even simple accidents like the spilling of a glass of water were subject to fines of two cents. In fact, says George, "There were never any accidents in those days —everything was assumed to be either intentional or excessively careless and deserving of a penalty." The Hall "tried in every way to prevent us from getting [any of our weekly allowance of ten cents] by a system of fines." George was often hard pressed to buy the weekly five-cent package of gum which "normally kept him and his girlfriend going over the weekend."

Evidence, were more evidence needed, that Newfoundland was in the grip of the Depression was daily provided by the Hall cooks. For breakfast, "You normally filled up with porridge and lassy bread — never once did I see bacon and eggs." By 'dinner' time at 12:30 the boys were famished but had to fill the aching void with "tough liver, which we called rubber heels, or some other kind of cheap meat or bad fish." The menu never varied. The tea was spurned as 'slops' because "it was mixed outside to take one taste off and put another on." Perhaps it was the Feild Hall fare, which made "indelible marks" on his stomach, that induced in the famished Change Islands lad his celebrated taste for good food and his hearty appetite. About the only food, aside from "bread and praties and gravy and beans," served in abundance was prunes. So, "We became experts at eating prunes — the record was fifty-six at one meal." Still, George later noted, "we all survived."

In his first year at Memorial College George took physics, for which summer school had well prepared him, economics, English, history and Latin. Among his second-

year courses, including one in education with Dr. Solomon
Whiteway, the highlights were Latin and Roman history
with J.L. Paton, Principal of the college, and English with
Alfred Hunter. Like most students who encountered Paton, George was always to regard meeting him as one of
the "great privileges" of his life. Paton was not only a
learned and inspiring teacher, but regularly invited students to his office and home. In an interview with Malcolm
MacLeod in 1983 (*Crossroads Country*), George offered this
portrait of his idol.

> He used to invite us up to his home. He looked like a
> bum in the way he dressed, very unassuming — you
> would never know who it was — his jacket was about
> twice too big for him, baggy trousers and all this. By and
> by you overlooked all that, because here were some
> going around dressed up like dolls you know, with not
> half as much inside; but he had it all inside and not much
> outside.

Typical of Paton's interest in individual students was
the fact that when he noticed that George had not regis-
tered for the second year, he sent a telegram to Fogo asking
why he was not returning. Informed that George had to
stay out for financial reasons, Paton wired back that he had
been awarded the Carnegie Scholarship for a second year
at the College. And so it was that the year 1932-33 found
George again at Memorial College instead of in the teaching job he had been hoping to find.

Dr. Hunter was another teacher George held in high
regard. But many students, George included, held him in
awe bordering on terror. Unnerved by Hunter's nasty
habit of springing questions on individual students,
George, trying to take advantage of his somewhat diminu-
tive form, always sought to hide behind the biggest chap

in class. But "old Hunter, as cute, my son, as a fox, was up to such ploys." "You hiding away behind that big fellow," often came the dreaded command, "what have *you* got to say on this question?" After the Reverend George Halden Earle returned from England in 1957 as Principal of Queen's College he and the stern inquisitor became friends, Earle often inviting him to lecture at the College.

George sometimes seemed to go out of his way to deny that he was ever a dedicated student, either in Change Islands or at Memorial. But while he didn't have the single-mindedness and brilliant record of his friend Mose Morgan, his performance certainly didn't justify his modesty. His one academic boast was that in his second year at Memorial College in an education class he topped his Fogo teacher Ted Russell, "a sweet experience" of which he had given Russell due warning. (After teaching in Fogo, Russell had returned to the College for his second year.) Aside from Russell, whose mischievous Jethro Noddy George would fifty years later portray on television, among George's forty-six classmates were, not surprisingly, a number of people who would become prominent in Newfoundland life, including H.M. Batten, W.J. Blundon, J.P. Higgins, Isaac Mercer, Isobel Moore and Rex Renouf.

Having settled on a teaching career, George called on I.J. Samson, the newly appointed superintendent of Church of England schools, to check on possibilities. But despite the fact that, as he told a Memorial University convocation in 1979, he was "filled to the rafters with learning," Samson could offer him nothing more than a promise to let him know should a vacancy occur anywhere in the country. The visit to Samson, so disappointing for George, was, incidentally, eventful for other people. While he was chatting with Ted Russell outside Samson's office his twenty-one-year-old cousin Dora Oake happened to

Graduation, Memorial University College, 1933.

come along. After being introduced to her, Russell, obviously struck by the accomplished young woman from Change Islands, turned to George, "Where have you been keeping *her* all this time?" "Away from you, boy," quipped George. George always took pleasure in the thought that without this chance meeting there might not have been a Russell-Oake wedding, or a Kelly Russell singing his songs and an Elizabeth editing the tales of Uncle Mose.

If his failure to find a job was frustrating, the thought of having to return home was mortifying. Not only would he be a financial burden to his family, but, filled to the rafters with learning, would have to brave the outport suspicion that much learning is apt to render a person useless anyway. Thus George could only have taken as a double-edged compliment the old Fogo codger's greeting, "I s'pose you can even talk sharthand now." Fortunately he didn't have long to skulk around the harbour. Later in the summer he received a pink telegram from Samson offering him a teaching position in Williamsport from September to December at $20 a month. Although it was clear that he would earn nothing beyond his board and a few dollars to repay his father for the fare, in late August he boarded the S.S. *Prospero* for the long journey across Notre Dame Bay and along the French Shore to Williamsport.

Williamsport, now abandoned, was one of Newfoundland's most isolated and deprived communities. Known as Greenspond (crews from Greenspond, Bonavista Bay having fished there) when it was settled in the 1890s, it was renamed after Governor Ralph Williams in 1911. When George taught there in 1933 the population was around 100, divided between Church of England people and 'Methodists.' In accordance with the churches' interests, if not with the pupils', the teachers were alternately of these two faiths. George was both teacher and lay reader. Coming from Change Islands and Fogo, he was struck by the economic and social deprivation of the people. Although the thought of becoming a clergyman had now and then occurred to him, it was the experience with poverty and despair in Williamsport that fixed his mind on the ministry as an instrument of the good works for which his uncle Canon J.T. Richards was already a legendary figure as rural dean in the Strait of Belle Isle. Thus the four months as a teacher in Williamsport turned out to be a pivotal experience. Half a century later, when Canon Earle was living in retirement in Topsail, he was accosted by a woman after a Sunday morning service, "Are you the Mr. Earle who once taught in Williamsport?" Assured that he was indeed the man, she told him, "Well, my husband is the pupil who won the prize you set up for the first student to learn the alphabet. He still has that five-cent piece and wouldn't part with it for anything." The first bread cast upon the waters had returned.

George's voyage home after his term ended turned out to be the first of several adventures he was to experience on the sea. The only means of travel in late December was the S.S. *Prospero* on her last trip north before the close of navigation. As it was unlikely that the vessel would call at Williamsport on the southbound trip, George boarded it on its way north. "So," the penny-conscious George was to boast, "I got a free trip nearly down to Cook's Harbour somewhere." The *Prospero* left Williamsport on December 20, spent Christmas Day in St. Anthony and arrived at Lewisporte on January 2. Having missed Christmas Day and New Year's, George anticipated being home for some festivities before Old Christmas Day.

Aside from the frustration of not being able to reach home for Christmas, for a 19-year-old the voyage was not without its attractions. "There were only three or four passengers, and the grub was plentiful, lots of it and the best kind. I was always famished at meal times, so I made the best of it." In recognition of the season the steward even kept a bowl of oranges on the saloon table. It was understood that for breakfast or for 'lunches' a passenger was welcome to as many oranges, perhaps three or four, as his taste called for. By a nice extension of that understanding, George reasoned that it would also be in order to hoard a few. For twelve days therefore he squeezed oranges into every space of his already bulging suitcase. For this liberal interpretation of ships' etiquette he was to pay a price. As he staggered across the deck of the *Prospero* in Lewisporte to join the *Clyde* for the trip to Fogo the hinges of his overburdened suitcase gave out. "Well, my-y-y son, oranges all over the deck, oranges goin' everywhere, rollin' around all over the place." Happening to be a witness, the Captain, "a gruff old feller, Captain Jacob Kean — used to skipper the *Home* and *Susu* — well he bellowed out, 'Did you steal these oranges?' 'No, sir, I sove 'em up'." The Captain didn't press the issue, but for a long time the young teacher's face remained red.

With his oranges retrieved and his suitcase tied up with twine, George made his escape from the *Prospero* and boarded the *Clyde* for the last leg of the long journey to Fogo. In less than an hour out of Lewisporte, off Michael's Harbour, the *Clyde* became stuck in the thick ice that had formed in that exceptionally early and cold winter of 1933-1934. Desperate now, George decided to walk to Fogo, over the ice when possible and along paths between communities otherwise, a distance of more than seventy miles. After taking a few necessities, including oranges, from his suitcase, which the *Clyde* would take back to Lewisporte for later delivery to Fogo by the mailman, George, Roy Dawe (a Fogo teacher) and lumberman Johnny Waterman of Change Islands took to the ice for the long trek eastwards. Sustained by the hospitality of homes they passed, and by pauses for an orange or two, they walked all night, reaching Boyd's Cove in time for an early breakfast, "the biggest kind," at the home of a Mrs. Pelly. That night, January 4, found the weary trio "sound sleep" in Port Albert, their last mainland stop. The next day, a bitterly cold and windy one, they made their way across the treacherous sea ice to the southwest tip of Change Islands, where Waterman left them, and thence on the "trickiest bit of ice of all" to the south end of Fogo Island, where they were met by George's father with horse and sleigh. "That," George reflected six decades later while rubbing his knees in arthritic pain, "is the stuff you could do when you were nineteen."

After repaying his father the fare he had borrowed for the trip to Williamsport, George had less than $10 to show for his four months of teaching. But his financial fortunes suddenly took a turn for the better. He had just arrived home when he was offered the school in Island Harbour, a tiny community on the north side of Fogo Island. Boarding with the Tom Bennett family, with "grub of the best kind and lots of card-playing," the winter passed very pleasantly.

Along with teaching, George conducted church services. His sermons were read from an approved collection, the Church of England being leery of laymen's theology. Finding these sermons too wordy, George was wont to edit them. But omitting sections soon proved to be a risky business. After one service he was accosted by an old parishioner, "You've been leaving out some of the stuff." Taken aback, George asked, "How do you know that?" "Because I watches your eyes droppin' from the top of the page to the bottom. Put it all in. We can choose if we wants to hear it or not." Thereafter George edited with more caution. A more serious problem with his Sunday Church duties was that they curtailed the weekend time he could spend with his girlfriend in Fogo, seven miles distant.

George was again lucky when for the year 1934-35 he was given the school in Seldom Come By, ten miles or so across the island from Fogo. Compared with Williamsport and Island Harbour, Seldom was a bustling community. Settled in the early 1800s, it boasted a population of over 300, a long-established school and a branch of the Fishermen's Union Trading Company (which promoted Art Scammell's Coaker engines). As one of the few safe harbours on the route from the more southerly bays to Labrador, Seldom enjoyed the status of a port of call for schooners and large boats. The put-put of Coaker engines "tied up with twine" complemented the silence of schooners at anchor. The bustle and excitement of the harbour evoked memories of the Change Islands George had left as a boy of fourteen. To top it all off, his salary had jumped from $20 a month to $25, while monthly board was only $10, compared with $12.50 in Williamsport.

Weekends saw George trudging across the island to see his girlfriend in Fogo. The walk over that desolate path normally took three hours. But in the dark of night or with the sun low in the western sky George cut the time by a third, for it was over this very road that Seldom's most notorious and feared ghost had chased a local bachelor. George was never one to write off ghosts as jack-o'-lanterns. When four decades later, in May 1976, he spoke at a Fogo Island High School dinner he was moved to recall memories of the ghost that had quickened his own pace. This he did in an eleven-verse ballad, "The Seldom Seen Ghost" (later published in his *Old Foolishness or Folklore?*). The essential facts are in six verses.

> In Seldom town there was a house, all white with
>   facings green,
> As nice a house as you would wish or may have ever
>   seen;
> But it lay empty for a year, which made the owner
>   weep,
> For it was haunted, people said, and so was going
>   cheap;
> So Jacob bought this empty house and soon began to
>   boast
> That he was scarified of nought — of devil, man or
>   ghost.

And so, as owner of a house, he asked her for her [his
    girlfriend's] hand
And when she quickly turned him down he couldn't
    understand;
But begging, coaxing, promising brought this condi-
    tion forth:
"If you're the man you think you are you thus must
    prove your worth:
Go sleep one night in that old house and if no ghost is
    seen
I'll promise that I'll marry you and be your faithful
    queen."

So, off he set with confidence that he would win his
    bride
And, feared of nothing, reached the house and soon
    was safe inside;
He snoffed his lantern in the porch and lit the bed-
    room lamp
And started up the creaky stairs and 'cross the hall did
    tramp;
But when he oped the bedroom door the draft
    blowed out the light
And, thar he wuz, surrounded by the phantoms of the
    night.

He took his tie and jacket off and lid down on the bed,
His socks and trousers would be next if all went well,
    he said;
He didn't dout the lamp as yet but only screwed en
    down
And then stretched out and listened to the sounds out
    in the town;
He must have dozed for when he looked, thar
    standin' be the post
Was sure enough, no doubt at all, a gurt big ugly
    ghost.

He didn't think, he didn't freeze, but off the bed he
   shoots
And out the door and down the stairs and in his
   rubber boots
And o'er the fence and up the road that leads across
   the isle,
A stretch of gravelled twisty road for near a dozen
   mile;
He ran as man had never run that road from coast to
   coast
'Cause man had not been chased before by Seldom's
   real ghost.

Right at the end of Sargeant's Cove, on past the
   Gravelly Knap,
An empty house enticed the ghost to quit this trying
   scrap;
He was too badly beaten out to go back o'er that road
And said he'd be contented here and took up his
   abode.
So Jacob left and spun his yarn and got his longed-for
   spouse
And Fogo got the Seldom ghost and got a haunted
   house.

Despite nerve-wracking hours in the dark of that
haunted road, the year in Seldom was a happy one. The
climax of the school year came in May when Seldom joined
hamlets, towns and cities throughout the Empire in celebrating the Silver Jubilee of George V. The school staged a
concert on May 6. One can fancy now the chairman's
announcing "the next item on the programme," which is
extant in George's handwriting.

1.   How do you do
2.   Play, "Country Cousins" — 1st Act
3.   Cowboy Song — Home on the Range

4.   Play—— 2nd Act
5.   In the Valley of the Moon
6.   Play — 3rd Act
7.   Rose of Tralee
8.   Uncle Pete
9.   Old MacDonald
10. The Man With Nerve
11. Danny Boy
12. Matrimony
13. Closing Chorus
14. The King

After pouring their emotions into this Empire gala, and with the sounds and smells of spring beckoning, the pupils must have been envious of the easy escape of wintered bluebottles and millers through the open windows. The teacher's mind had already turned to a new career.

In September 1935 George began study for the ministry at Queen's College as one of about a dozen students. At College George already showed the penchant for the doggerel that would always be a favored vehicle of his wit and humour. Two of his humorous poems, his first publications, appeared in *Live Wire*, the College paper, which he edited, in the fall of his second year at Queen's. A few sample verses will convey the tone. From "Are We Idle? No," an account of students' summer employment:

> Ralph (to speak of him is risky)
> Is as brave as Captain Guy;
> With his daddy journeyed Northward,
> Rather daring for a boy.
> Eddie Parsons (Social standing
> Didn't come into his brain)
> Worked at Murray's with the Shoremen;
> Fish and oil in sun and rain.

Pike, who should consult a dentist,
Took a job on Water Street,
Went about for Mr. Harvey,
Wore big blisters on his feet.
Wareham, loving great adventure,
Took a trip out on the Banks,
Spent his time (instead of fishing)
Viewing lice and bugs at pranks.

Earle, who came in late as usual,
Tells about his five-mile walk
To his little school so tiny,
Teaching Fogo how to talk.
Fowlow, that great daring viking,
Bald, adventurous and brave,
Sought the fish among the Huskies
In the 'Gov'nor of the Wave.'

And from "Constructive Criticism," observations on
his classmates' foibles and physical peculiarities:

Things of late have come before us
Of this student body here;
Jokes and fun have oft arisen,
No one yet has shed a tear.
Tender spots have sure been touched sir,
Clearly shown upon the face
Of the boys from Harbour Buffett,
Trinity and Harbour Grace.

Batten gifted (that's quite obvious)
With long legs and neck and nose;
Gets ahead of Legge and Kirby,
In his place he doth repose.
Walter Raleigh had a garment,
On it walked good Queen Bess;
Batten's sweater, room for camels
In a lonely wilderness.

Wareham, senior man by proxy,
Is an asset, none will doubt.
Leads the singing; and the reading,
When the leading man is out.
Realizing that the students
Are mixed up in race and clime,
Compromises with an accent
He acquired with work and time.

Earle, who takes his place by Alton,
Tries to sing, but what a sound;
Even drowns the voice of Dickey;
(When the voices meet they bound).
On his left the moon is shining,
Batten's sweater is the sky.
When he sees the two together,
Laugh he does like any boy.

In the spring of 1937 George passed the General Ordination Examination set by the Church in England, but elected to defer the office of deacon, taking a third year of study to qualify for the L.Th. from the University of Durham, with which Queen's had been affiliated for about twenty-five years. He was made deacon in June 1938.

A Coastal Mission

George spent the early summer of 1938 at home in Fogo, where he preached his first sermon as deacon. On the text "Be ye followers of God," it was orthodox in theology, churchy and unquestioning, but the new deacon was pleased enough with it that he chose to give it as his first sermon a year later in England. In 1956, however, the year before he returned from England, he wrote across its first page, "my first two attempts at preaching as a deacon — of souvenir value only." While in Fogo in the early summer he received a telegram from Co-adjutor Bishop Abraham appointing him Chaplain for the Bishop's summer visit to parishes from Curling to Seldom Come By on the Church boat *Argonaut*. This visit to "all Anglican, i.e. Christian communities," as he quipped to a dissenting friend, was but one of the experiences that justified his later claiming deep and wide knowledge of Newfoundland's history and culture.

The new deacon left Fogo for Corner Brook on the S.S. *Clyde* on July 12, meeting the Bishop at the Glynmill Inn the next day. On Glynmill letterhead he outlined his duties for the trip. As much those of a ship's executive officer as of a chaplain, they included the arranging and updating of schedules, paying the crew of two, paying for the boat's supplies, recording expenses (including his $11.35 fare from Fogo to Humbermouth) as well as recording offerings to the Bishop's Visitation Fund. This business, along with accounts of the Bishop's visit to each of the thirty-six parishes, is meticulously recorded in a ninety-page diary. (A three-part summary of the diary was published in 1989 and 1990 in the *Newfoundland Quarterly*.) Almost all of the parishes visited were fishing communities, where the Depression had left people in pitiful economic and social conditions. The average income of inshore fishermen was about $200, about 52,000 people were still on the dole, while upwards of ninety percent of children were suffering from malnutrition. The observed need for practical assistance, which had first moved George in Williamsport, quickened his interest in the muscular or practical Christianity exemplified by his uncle, Canon Richards, and two years later dictated his choice of a curacy in England.

While the *Argonaut* was still en route from St. John's in stormy weather the Bishop conducted confirmation services in the new Corner Brook Church (now Cathedral) of St. John the Evangelist and, by means of a boat provided by Will and Frank Brake of Meadows, in communities around the Bay. The beauty of the Bay moved the son of bleak Change Islands to record, "Going down the Bay was beautiful....Mt. Moriah towered out in its beauty on the left. Summerside and Meadows on the right presented a beauty of nature. Everything was so green and beautiful." He was inspired by the confirmation services at John's Beach in the tiny school/chapel built by the Reverend Uricus Zwinglius Rule in 1866-67 and reputed to be the oldest church in the Bay. After forty-eight parishioners, some from Frenchman's Cove, McIver's and Woods Island, "received the gift of the Holy Spirit," the Bishop and Chaplain returned to a hospitable home where "we enjoyed our first treat of strawberries and cream." This is but one of many scoffs and feasts George recorded that summer, his physical hunger always matching his spiritual thirst.

While heading out the Bay to Lark Harbour later that day of July 14, they passed Governor Island where the *Lavrock*, the church ship of many years ago, was wrecked. Presented to the church in 1872 after it had suffered the loss of an earlier boat, this yacht, formerly the *Skylark*, conveyed clergymen, including three bishops, on missions along the treacherous coasts until a storm claimed it in 1909. (Had the Bishop and Chaplain been able to see a few weeks ahead, they would have been filled with foreboding about the *Lavrock*'s fate.) A confirmation service was held at St. James's Church, Lark Harbour at 6:30. One of the two decorated arches on the road to the Church had the inscription WELCOME TO HER LORDSHIP. Cryptically George observed, "but the HER is not so irrelevant after all." No fewer than seventy-three people were confirmed in the "beautifully adorned" church. As was his practice on the voyage, George noted that bodily needs were also generously provided for. At the home of Mr. and Mrs. M.G. Sheppard he had "a supper second to none in every way." And before he went to bed at 11:30 he enjoyed "a refreshing drink of milk" — a rare luxury in the outports of the time.

The trip out the Bay and around Black Head to Cox's Cove in "just enough lop for enjoyment" was more tranquil than the community scene that greeted the Bishop. As his boat was docking in the Cove a cutter pulled in with three police officers, a ranger and a magistrate to quell a disorderly demonstration against the Island Timber Company, which was producing pit-props in the community. But the confirmation service was "done decently and in order," eighteen people being confirmed. The atmosphere in Cox's Cove was in sharp contrast with the pastoral tranquillity of Meadows later that evening. The next morning, Saturday, July 16 the Bishop returned to Curling.

Meanwhile the *Argonaut* had arrived at Curling after a rough and slow trip from St. John's, and was ready to take the Bishop's party north through the Strait of Belle Isle and southward into Notre Dame Bay. The *Argonaut*, at twelve tons, was not exactly a commodious boat for four people on such a long voyage, one of them a six-foot five inch bishop. Worse still, the twelve horsepower, two-cylinder Acadia engine, like most gas engines of the time, was subject to fits of crankiness, sometimes refusing to start and often breaking down. The engineer, Roy Legge, certainly earned his $22.50 per month, while Skipper John Wiseman well deserved his $25. As for George, he "never wanted to lay his eyes on the likes of that engine again." A kind of yawl, the *Argonaut* had been consecrated as a church ship in St. John's in June, the month George was made deacon.

The *Argonaut* slipped her lines at Curling just after noon on Monday, July 18 headed for Trout River. Turning north at Woods Island she immediately ran into turbulent seas. "The teapot and water jug were on the floor...butter on locker, cutlery on floor, and nothing anywhere in particular but everywhere in general." It was 'fun' observing the Bishop trying to eat his first lunch at sea — fun for a Change Islander if not for the Bishop from Staffordshire via Nottingham and Quebec City. Although they found Trout River "rent with schism," twenty-six parishioners were confirmed, some of them from the isolated tiny community of Chimney Cove. It was of great interest to Deacon Earle that it was from Chimney Cove, a mere notch in the towering cliffs, that young Fred Buffett had gone out into the world to become a Church of England rector in Devon, England. In 1939 Buffet published a short history of the Newfoundland Church, which included a photograph of the *Argonaut* at a St. John's wharf on the day of her consecration. (It was for Otto Tucker and me a moving experience in the summer of 1984 to chat with this urbane cleric and prize-winning flower gardener from a barren Newfoundland cove on the beautiful lawn of his retirement home in Newton Abbot, Devon.)

Heading north from Trout River late on Friday, July 18, the *Argonaut* spent the next three days in Bonne Bay, where confirmation services were held in Birchy Head, Lomond, Norris Point, Rocky Harbour and Woody Point. At Woody Point Deacon Earle received an interesting greeting from the incumbent, Tobias Short, who had taught him in Change Islands in 1927-28. He "informed me that I was then an imp. . . . Now I am a parson, but I hope my impishness within bounds will not be lost." This was but the first of several of George's comments that can be interpreted as concern about the length of rein a clergyman should give to his humour.

Of one of the communities in Bonne Bay he wrote, "Far too much beer is consumed around here" and this probably explains why "the collection of $2.98 was disappointing." In each of the sixty churches from Curling to Seldom an offering was taken for the Bishop's Visitation Fund. These offerings were a reliable measure of the 'cash flow' of parishioners and a fair, though less accurate, indication of the people's economic straits. The three smallest offerings were $0.35, $0.40 and $1.18. The average, even when boosted by $14.01 at Corner Brook, $13.80 at Woody Point, $16.89 at Twillingate and a high of $20.48 at Joe Batt's Arm, was only $3.10. Newfoundland fishing communities had always been striking examples of how hope for economic betterment can be sustained in chronic poverty. In Bonne Bay George found some people looking to the tuna sports–fishery popularized by Lee Wulff as the "economic future" of the Bay. Indeed Wulff, as an adviser to the government on tourism in the area, was tuna fishing in the Bay when the *Argonaut* arrived.

On Friday, July 22, at 8 a.m. the *Argonaut* slipped her lines from the Woody Point wharf and headed north to Sally's Cove. "It was a marvellous day with bright sun and a fresh breeze; surely God is with us on this trip, for immediately before the Visitation the weather was terrible." As Sally's Cove had no harbour, the Bishop and Deacon were ferried to the beach in a small boat. In stepping from the boat to the rocks, the episcopal diary records, "the Bishop tore his breeches and later had to sit in a parlour on a cushion with the comforting words YOU ARE THE DAISY OF MY HEART." From these mortifying experiences the Bishop rallied to confirm eighteen parishioners, including a grandmother, mother and daughter.

The *Argonaut*, under sail now, was off to Cow Head by 12:30. "Guns were firing as we were rowed ashore and while we walked to the parsonage." The confirmation service was held at 7:15 in the school/chapel, which boasted a new "lobster organ," so called because, in lieu of cash, the admission charged to a concert to raise money for it was a bucket of lobsters. In one of his expressions of deep admiration for the ingenuity of outporters, George added "How some men have the ability to use the means at their disposal." Delayed by southwest wind and fog, the Bishop also conducted Evensong the next day. Anticipating an overflow for the service, parishioners were seen wending their way to church with chairs on their backs. Although George had kept a heavy lid on his always simmering humour, it bubbled over at this sight.

> No time here my boys to be slack
> For seats the school-chapel does lack;
> Just stroll off to prayers
> Without any fears
> And place your seat upon your back.

After this touch of irreverence, the next sentence reads, "Evensong was wonderful, as deep and impressive a one as I ever attended."

On Wednesday, July 27 the *Argonaut* resumed its northerly course. After services in Parson's Pond and Portland Creek, the next stop was Daniel's Harbour, where the organist for the confirmation service was Myra Bennett, who as nurse Grimsley had come from London to Daniel's Harbour in 1921 and who is now celebrated as "Nurse Bennett," her many honours including the M.B.E. and the Order of Canada. The next stop was Belburns, where George was struck by the quality and relative financial well-being of the people. "This place is different from others. Houses large and well kept up. Hard working people — never stop. The people for the most part are House by name." Eight people were confirmed. Bishop Abraham's sermon topic, "Daily Increase," seemed aptly chosen.

That night, Thursday, July 28, found the *Argonaut* at a secure berth in Port Saunders, the best harbour north of Bonne Bay and one of the few good ones on the coast. The next day, after church service, the cook/captain prepared "an excellent dinner" to mark the Bishop's forty-first birthday. If food was always a treat for George, tobacco was a necessity. In Cow Head he had lamented the "shortage of baccy" when high winds prevented his replenishing his supply from the *Argonaut* at anchor. Now, at Port Saunders, he had the misfortune to break his pipe. While walking back from the post office "I broke my $1.20 Flyweight pipe. What a break!" But once again the ingenuity of outporters came to his rescue, when Reg Taylor, his host, "put a .44 bullet shell on for a ferrule."

Following the noon birthday feast, the *Argonaut* resumed her cruise north but, unable to round Point Riche in the stiff southwesterly, had to return to Port Saunders. The evening was spent salmon fishing in Hawke's Bay. Although salmon were "jumping up the falls by the dozens," none were landed. But the trip did afford the Bishop and George the peculiar pleasure of spending a night, their first, on the *Argonaut*. After dinner, which featured French-fried potatoes, a luxury not then common in Newfoundland, a pleasant evening was passed in Evensong in the cramped cabin, listening to the BBC, then the chief source of international news, and enjoying "a few smokes." After the wind abated calls were made at Shoal Cove West, Brig Bay, Current Island and Anchor Point.

George's diary for Sunday, July 31 begins, "Arose at 7:15 with a mighty bad stomach which I suspected as 'this here summer complaint.'" With the *Argonaut* fogbound at Anchor Point, he forced himself to walk the six miles to Flower's Cove and the comfort of the parsonage with Uncle Tom and Aunt Dora (his mother's sister) Richards. Aunt Dora immediately dosed him with wine and aspirin and sent him to bed. The next day, now in the grip of "terrible cuttin pains," he felt even worse. The deprived gourmand scribbled, "Still not well, but suffering more by not being able to eat the 'good stuff' than from my complaint." And once again he couldn't resist a bit of doggerel.

You suffer a lot from a pain in the belly,
But more when you can't eat the cake and the jelly.
On the table before you a pot roasted chicken
But not on your life do you dare even 'lick en.'

You stare at the good stuff that's made by Aunt DO
Your mouth and eyes water — your stomach says NO!
I'd rather have boils, and occasionally faint
Than that terrible illness — 'The Summer Complaint.'

On the third day he was not only suffering but becoming worried. "A bad day with awfully bad stomach, almost enough to worry about." Fortunately, as it turned out, he had only one more day of the 'complaint' ahead of him.

While at Flower's Cove the *Argonaut* incurred a variety of expenses, including: 5 lbs. of cork at 35 cents, 3 yards of canvas at 66, 19 gallons of gas at $7.60 (40 cents a gallon being five cents more than the usual price), 24 batteries at $10.80 and 1 gallon of kerosene for the lamp at 38 cents. In addition, an engine part had to be repaired. For this work, the two local men submitted a revealing invoice:

> Dear Rev. Sir,
>
> We helped engineer to fix piece for engine. He advised to send the bill to you, which is 25c. If this is OK please deliver same to the bearer of this note.
>
> > we remain
> >
> > Your's Humbly.

On Thursday, August 4 the *Argonaut* crossed the Strait of Belle Isle for confirmation services at L'Anse au Clair, L'Anse au Loup and Forteau, then part of the Flower's Cove Mission. Among the eight people confirmed at L'Anse au Clair was a severely disabled woman who was confirmed in her seat, "a sad sight as the women burst into crying and I myself could not refrain from expressing my deep emotion in that way." Reflection at Forteau on the work of another deacon, A. Gifford, who in 1849 established the first church there, also stirred George's emotions. "On an emotion such as I then experienced," he wrote after citing facts about Gifford's service, "I would do anything for Christ, fired as I was by the fiery zeal and profound devotion of Mr. Gifford." On the return trip across the Strait the crew enjoyed "a fine tea" of puffins shot by the Bishop.

Strong southwest wind kept the *Argonaut* tied up at Flower's Cove for the next two days. As there was little the

Bishop, Canon and Chaplain could do outdoors, they spent the two days chatting, reading, and enjoying Aunt Dora's wonderful 'scoffs,' "especially the strawberries and cream." Such a close association with two older clergymen, each distinguished in his own sphere, was a rich experience for a green young deacon of twenty-four. Bishop Abraham, an Englishman born in the cathedral city of Lichfield, a graduate of Eton and Oxford, consecrated at Lambeth Palace, brought to the isolated outport parsonage English speech and values, the learning of Oxford and the prestige of Canterbury; while Uncle Tom Richards, appointed rural dean of the Strait of Belle Isle the year George was born, was already enjoying the acclaim, perhaps partly through his long association with Sir Wilfred Grenfell, that would make him a kind of legend in Newfoundland. Half a century after this stormbound sojourn with Uncle Tom, George, after lauding such churchmen as U.Z. Rule and Joseph Curling, wrote, "Now I was in the presence of another of equal stature." (*Newfoundland Quarterly*, December 1989). For his forty years of work for Strait communities Canon Richards was awarded an O.B.E. in 1949.

Sunday morning, August 7 brought clear skies and a light northwesterly. The *Argonaut* left before 7 a.m. for the long haul to Cook's Harbour, meeting the *Empress of Britain* en route. "Troubled with engine and a leak in the stuffing box but ploughed along." The next day's trip across Pistolet Bay to Raleigh must have stirred memories of singing in more tranquil scenes for those in peril on the sea. The *Argonaut* was ploughing into a northeasterly, the sea made more turbulent by a contrary tide. To add to the concern, the engine was again acting up and the stuffing box was leaking badly. "What a mess." It was a relieved crew who docked at Raleigh in freshening wind just before noon. George spent the afternoon helping to install a new stuffing box. But by 7:30 he was ready for the confirmation service. Of Raleigh George noted that a "fine lot of fish was caught here this summer;" and that, thankfully, the community would soon get its first Church of England teacher, "as all the time our children have gone to a Methodist school" — not a comment he would have made about church schools fifty years later.

Had the crew known the extent of engine troubles while punching into yesterday's northeasterly they would have been even more anxious. It was discovered in the morning that the bearings had burnt out. As this problem could not be corrected anywhere nearer than St. Anthony the *Argonaut* departed Raleigh for Quirpon under sail. By prearrangement they were met at Quirpon by Esau Hillier of Griquet in his *Peerless* for the long tow to Griquet and thence to St. Anthony. Although "guns firing incessantly" greeted the Bishop at Griquet he entered the harbour "not exactly in the most dignified manner."

At 7:15 a.m., August 10, the *Peerless* headed out into a northeasterly swell towing not only the *Argonaut* but the rudderless *Miss Newfoundland*. The *Miss Newfoundland* was the best known boat in outports of the time. Owned by Gerald S. Doyle, she took him around the bays each summer soliciting orders for such thin-blood and nerve remedies as cod liver oil, Brick's Tasteless and Beef, Iron and Wine (also found beneficial by men short of moonshine). Next to the Sunday School picnic, her arrival was a summer highlight for youngsters, for, known as the Bloom Boat in some communities, she always handed out free balloons, "one to a child." Sharing the shame with the *Argonaut*, she was now approaching the St. Anthony government wharf a cripple. Both boats could have done without the guns firing, foghorns blowing and "bells ringing somewhere," but they were soon in the dry dock and out of sight of the multitudes gathered to greet the Bishop.

It turned out that the *Argonaut's* troubles were worse than feared. "Shaft plied a lot and both stuffing boxes broken. The blades were plied slightly, having struck a bolt in the rudder." For repairs the invoice, to His Lordship The Bishop of Newfoundland, neatly typed on International Grenfell Association (Marine Railway Dock) letterhead totalled $25.37. Yet the invoice was receipted "in full for $1.97" (for a copper rod), the amount also entered in George's ledger. Perhaps the dock manager was a good Church of England man.

Confirmation service was held in St. Mary's church on the evening of the Bishop's "less than dignified" arrival at St. Anthony. The next day while the *Argonaut* was in dry dock the Bishop and Earle in a local boat visited Ireland Bight, where nine people were confirmed. On their return to St. Anthony at 8 p.m. they found that *Miss Newfoundland* had quietly slipped out into the night. The *Argonaut* itself was ready to sail the next morning. After taking on such necessities as gasoline and meat, and for "spot cash" the luxuries of a bottle of vinegar (35 cents), a hair brush ($1.20) and a nail brush (30 cents), she headed into stormy waters for Williamsport halfway down the French Shore. In the heavy southeast wind and with a big sea running, it was "too rough either to cook or lay table." In fact at six o'clock the captain had to alter course for Crouse. Following 'tea' at 8 p.m. the windy evening was passed in listening to the BBC. The headlines for that evening (August 12) were that about 500 Chinese had been killed in a skirmish with Japanese troops, the S.S. *Queen Mary* had beaten a speed record, logging an average of over 31 knots on a day's run, and the Duke and Duchess of Gloucester had travelled to Egypt, mostly by air, on a holiday. The evening ended at eleven o'clock with Evensong, as it always did when the Bishop slept aboard.

South-bound the next morning, the *Argonaut* passed six schooners that had left Crouse earlier in the morning "in good style and beauty," including the *Lloyd Jack, Melba, Fog Free Zone* and *Uronick*. A little later off Cape Fox they passed *Miss Newfoundland* of unhappy memory. As the *Argonaut*, now under sunny skies, rounded Fourché Point for Williamsport Earle felt that he was "going home," for it was here he had taught in 1933 and here he had committed himself to the ministry. His log names the many people he visited, and expresses delight in seeing the children he had taught. So joyously was he welcomed that the Bishop remarked "It's a pity you can't take Confirmation as I don't seem to be needed here." Five people were confirmed in a two o'clock service. From Williamsport the Bishop went on to Harbour Deep for an evening service in this solidly Anglican parish. During the service, Earle sadly noted, "Great coughing was experienced, among the children especially, real T.B. coughs."

Early the next morning, Sunday, August 14, George logged, "Very bright morning, which always looks suspicious." The suspicion of the experienced mariner was fully justified by mid-morning when the *Argonaut* found herself punching into White Bay in the teeth of an increasing southerly gale. With the boat sometimes burying her bowsprit in cresting seas, and averaging only three knots an hour, George himself was at the wheel for four and a half hours. It took good seamanship not to ship green water over the rounded bow. It was with a sense of accomplishment and relief that the wet and hungry crew found refuge in Jackson's Arm in the late afternoon of that black Sunday. A confirmation service was held at 7 p.m. in the large and splendid Church of St. Bartholomew "beautifully decorated with evergreens and flowers." Community pride in this "beautiful house of God" was palpable. The hymn "When the clouds unfold their wings of strife" might not have been suitable for a confirmation service, but on that stormy Sunday evening the mariners would have sung it with quickened emotions.

The next morning the *Argonaut* punched up the Bay against the strong southerly for services at Sops Island and Job's Cove, reaching Hampden at the bottom of the Bay after dark. Anticipating heading out the Bay the next morning with the wind behind them, the crew spent a relaxed night in Hampden. But it is the way of winds to chop and veer with changes in a vessel's course. Thus the log for that day, Tuesday, August 16, begins, "Arose at 6:15 a.m. What a disappointment. We have had head winds all the way up the Bay and did hope to have a 'freer' sail along. Bless me if the wind didn't veer about 6:30 to N.E., bringing heavy rain and fog. Another punch indeed facing us." The trip to Westport, a four-hour run from Hampden, turned out to be even worse than the southerly punch, "a nasty trip along with rain, fog and wind." The *Argonaut* docked at Westport at 12:45 p.m. It was on good evidence that the next morning in Westport George wrote his father that although the *Argonaut* was under-powered for head winds she was "a good sea boat."

At Westport the Bishop and George were hosted by "no less a personage" than the Reverend Christopher Wood, at 83 believed to be the oldest Anglican clergyman in Newfoundland, a half legendary character in the young chaplain's mind. From Westport George wrote his father, "Staying with Rev. C. Wood here now, who is still smart and remembers Fogo and Change Islands well." As a young boy in Change Islands George had relished the legend that it was the iron command of Wood and school-teacher Mr. Stone in Fogo in the 1880s that inspired the missionary hymn, "The heathen in his blindness/Bows down to wood and stone." Now, a half a century later, he was enjoying the lavish hospitality of this "Saintly (but frank) man of God." The ambience of the "cosy abode" of the former Cambridge student was more that of a Cotswolds cottage than an outport home. The sumptuous 'tea' of fresh salmon, with vegetables from the "kitchen garden," the fine wines and the pungent Stilton cheese ("I thought a cat had misbehaved under the table until Mr. Wood lifted the cover to reveal the cheese.") and cigars were all graciously served by the 'maid' of fourteen years, Mrs. Luke Gillingham.

After dinner, while the guests, especially George, were enjoying their cigars, an "inspiring evening of music" was enjoyed, Mr. Wood first treating the guests to classical music from his extensive collection of gramophone records, and later playing his Estey organ. (The organ, later bequeathed to Queen's College, was still being used in chapel services forty years later when Canon Earle retired as Provost.) In further evidence of his generosity, Mr. Wood augmented the collection of $3.62 at the afternoon confirmation service by a donation of $1.00.

Leaving this haven of comfort and luxury, the next morning the pilgrims departed in rain and fog for services at Bear Cove and Seal Cove. On the following afternoon, Thursday, August 18, the *Argonaut* rounded Partridge Point for the long run to Round Harbour, Notre Dame Bay, where an evening confirmation service was held. Attending the service was Mose Morgan, George's friend from Feild Hall days, who was working in nearby Tilt Cove on a geological survey. Their paths would take many sharp turns before the two friends became close associates, Mose as President of Memorial University and George as Provost of Queen's College.

That evening as the sun was sinking below the towering hills, the Bishop, George and others were taken in boat to nearby Tilt Cove to visit its monuments to change and decay. A mining community from 1869, Tilt Cove once boasted all 'modern' conveniences, four churches and three schools serving a population of over 1300. Now, on that August evening of 1938, the mine having been abandoned for twenty years, fewer than fifty people, including six Anglicans, lived among the ruins. A twilight visit to the graveyard "clearly showed that the greatest population of Tilt Cove were its dead." George's expression of emotion on entering the Anglican Church is an elegy in prose. The church, once "second to none in the outports of Newfoundland," now an abandoned ruin and leaking badly, had been prefabricated in England around 1870, its pulpit and pews were made of solid oak, "beautiful carpets covered the floors of the sanctuary and chancel," while the "exquisite east window would bring forth a prayer from anyone." The organ's "ancient beauty of sound," spared the ravage of time and rain, only added to the poignancy of the scene. "A deserted church in a deserted village," George concluded, "is a heartbreaking spectacle." It was a sombre procession that made its way back to the rickety dock for the dark trip back to Round Harbour.

Over the next three days the Bishop conducted confirmation services in Nippers Harbour, Little Bay, Leading Tickles and Exploits. With Nippers Harbour overrun by 'Methodists' or "the other crowd" (as George always liked to call evangelicals), only a handful of people attended the service, including a Henry Middleton who had arrived from Somerset fifty years before. The collection for the Bishop's Visitation Fund was thirty-five cents. Little Bay, the most beautiful setting encountered, "with level meadows, marvellous trees and clean, high hills," had only four Church of England households, including the families of Thomas and Augustus Wells and James Lind. But the Bishop, perhaps inspired by the environment, "never spoke deeper," and a generous offering of $3.30 was taken. The *Argonaut* left later in the afternoon, Friday, August 19, on the scenic trip west of Little Bay Islands, through Long Tickle and across Badger Bay to Leading Tickles, its next port of call, by-passing the larger non-Anglican or, as Canon Earle later quipped, non-Christian communities of Little Bay Islands, Pilley's Island and Triton. The next morning the Leading Tickles cemetery was consecrated in torrential rain. Back at the Church of St. Nicholas by noon, the Bishop in "damp garb" confirmed twenty-nine parishioners.

At 2:30 in the strongest winds yet encountered, a northwesterly, "lops breaking incessantly," the *Argonaut* rounded New Bay Head, a stretch of bald headland later dubbed Cape Horn by the skipper of the Pilley's Island vessel *Primrose II* because of the turbulence of wind and tide. But the *Argonaut* again proved her seaworthiness, and docked in the shallow harbour of Exploits at suppertime. Taking advantage of the storm delay, the Bishop conducted several services over the next twenty-four hours; and George replenished the vessel's supplies with a tin of Dutch Cleanser (16 cents) and two cans of lobster at forty cents each, and expended the large sum of $2.00 for laundry. When the *Argonaut* left Exploits at 2:30 (August 22) for Twillingate she had an additional passenger, the Rev. E.J. Simpson, Principal of Queen's College and, as it would turn out, a predecessor of Canon George Halden Earle.

Although the northwesterly gale had abated, there was a "good tumble" rounding Twillingate Long Point, as there usually is, but the welcome in the Capital of the North more than made up for it. Sixteen people were confirmed in an evening service in St. Peter's Church, while an offering of $13.39 augmented the Bishop's Fund. Combined with the evening offering the next morning's collection of $3.50 allowed St. Peter's to boast the 'grandest' total to date, topping Corner Brook's $14.01. Over the next two days the Bishop conducted confirmation services in several communities, including Herring Neck, Boyd's Cove and Pikes Arm. Important though these visits were for the church, for George they led back to Change Islands, the mecca of culture and religion, the home of saints and sleveens. It was therefore with anticipation and pride that he took the helm of the *Argonaut* for the approach to home waters. There was wind, fog and a big sea running, he recorded, "but as pilot I put her through." "It was good to be back in St. Margaret's where I was christened in 1914 and confirmed in 1926." His family came over from Fogo for the confirmation service. Every spare minute was given to meeting and "putting burdens on the digestive system" with relatives, and in visiting old friends, including young Bernard Thomas Scammell, whom George would next meet in wartime England.

The Bishop's pilgrimage would have fittingly ended in mecca. But lesser shrines awaited him. And so on Monday, August 29, the *Argonaut* in a strong southwesterly slipped her lines for Fogo. "I was so-called pilot to Fogo," George proudly noted, "so took charge with *Argonaut* under sail going before a good breeze." Even though, as he later remarked, Fogo "sometimes suffered from being too big in its boots," he had gone to school there after 1928 and it was now his family's home. He therefore relished the welcome of "guns exploding" and "cannons roaring." A very large congregation attended the evening service in which forty-seven people were confirmed. During a joyous reunion at his parents' home that evening he "enjoyed a couple of cigars given by Uncle Arthur" before going to bed at 12:30. The day's log ends, "Of course I am home again where sleep before midnight is unknown among the adults of our family."

After Fogo several more communities were visited, including Joe Batt's Arm. The Bishop's last service was held at Seldom on the dark, rainy evening of Friday, September 2. St. Augustine's Church, beautifully decorated with evergreens and pond lilies, was an oasis of cheer in a dark landscape. Eight people were confirmed and collection of $2.51 taken. Following the service and a "fine lunch" the Bishop, planning an early morning departure for St. John's, retired to the *Argonaut*. Later George, braving the rain and memories of the Seldom Seen Ghost, went aboard to bid farewell to the Bishop and crew. "Saw the last of the ship and her fine crew, and the Bishop with whom I had spent the happiest and most inspiring summer of my life."

The *Argonaut* experience was indeed an extraordinary one for a young bayman of twenty-four. It increased his knowledge and deepened his insight into the outport character about which he would write and speak as Canon George Earle; through close observation of poverty and consequent hardship, it reinforced his commitment to Uncle Tom Richards' practical Christianity; it gave him, through the Bishop's eyes, a glimpse of the "more mature and human" church in England; and whetted his appetite for the learning and worldly sophistication of his shipmate from Staffordshire, Eton and Oxford.

The War Years In England

After a brief holiday in Fogo, George returned to Queen's College to study for a licentiate in theology. At the same time he taught Latin at the College, assisted at the Cathedral and "ran errands" for the Bishop. In February (1939) he informed his parents that the Bishop had come to the College to show his movies of the summer voyage. "They were good, and I look fine in the movies," he told them in an assessment of his screen presence that the CBC's Jethro Noddy would portray almost fifty years later. In the same letter he told the family that he had just been accepted at St. Chad's College, University of Durham, in a one year study that would qualify him for the B.A. degree.

Meanwhile, in the spring he was chosen one of two Newfoundland delegates to a Christian Youth Conference of seventy nations in Amsterdam. For this lengthy detour from his trip to England the local Conference Committee, headed by the Reverend Wilfred Butcher of Queen's Road Presbyterian Church (the Kirk), gave him $50.00. Toward his costs at Durham his mother gave him $100 from the nest egg she had reserved for the children's education, and the church "scrounged around and found $25." He had just over $200 in his pocket when in early July at Bell Island, two days after his ordination as priest, he boarded the Dutch ore ship *Themisco* for Rotterdam.

As the voyage on the *Argonaut* showed, George enjoyed a schoolboy appetite. By dinnertime on the first day
at sea on the *Themisco* he was 'famished.' As the handful of
passengers sat at the Captain's table the steward presented
them with a small plate of beans. "I tucked in, and when
the beans were gone I was still famished. So I wondered to
the steward if I could have a few more. 'Oh yes, certainly
sir.' Well, my son, here I was on my seconds while the
other passengers were already into the second course.
Shockin'." From then on George was delighted to know
that in the outside world the first course, even beans, is not
the last one. After a stormy crossing the *Themisco* reached
Rotterdam about a week later. Taking a train to Amsterdam, George arrived at the Conference a day late. Semi-
nars were held and lectures given to the 1500 delegates by
eminent church scholars and leaders from around the
world. Among the excursions was a trip to the German
border where George observed goose-stepping soldiers
who, in less than a month, would be at war, changing the
course of his own life.

When the Conference was over George, his pockets
virtually empty, crossed the Channel to London. As his
study at Durham was not to begin until October he had
taken a month's locum in Silksworth, near Newcastle, in
relief of the holidaying vicar. The train trip from London
north to Newcastle afforded him his first glimpse of "all
that cultivated land, cultivated for centuries" and his first
encounter with Englishmen in their own milieu. The gregarious Newfoundlander was surprised that none of the
eight people in his train compartment cared to engage in
conversation with him. "Everyone was reading a paper or
looking up at the ceiling. I thought 'This is queer — home
we'd be chatting by now'." Partly as a strategy to get the
taciturn Englishmen to talk, and partly from Newfoundland custom George passed around his package of Ches-

terfield cigarettes. Three people deigned to accept the offer from a stranger. "Oh," said one, "I didn't know that you were a foreigner." To which the gregarious and cheeky Newfoundlander replied, "Well, you could have known an hour ago if you had opened your mouth." After that "they all became chatty and friendly."

While at Silksworth George received a visit from the principal of St. Chad's College. Asked to confirm that he was entering the College in October, George expressed some doubt that he could find the £40 fee payable on registration. "How much money do you have?" "Very little. Most of the money I have I can see by faith." When the principal observed, "That's not much help," George replied, "No, but it's a good start." Considering this attitude "very noble," the principal forthwith offered George the proctorship at St. Chad's. News of this windfall was conveyed to brother Fred a day or two later, September 19.

> Boy, something else has come my way which sticks me up a little bit higher. The Principal of St. Chad's College came to see me and informed me that he is placing me on the staff of St. Chad's College. It mightn't sound much but it means a lot. In the first place, it gives me board and lodging free, thus saving about £70 or $370, which is very good. Then it places me in a position to mix with big bugs and so gain good experience.... I believe God has led me to this and will lead me on.

The year in St. Chad's residence for pre-theology students turned out to be a rich experience. While as proctor and an ordained priest George had to keep some distance from the students, it was in his nature to be one of the boys. Stretching the truth a bit, he told them that he had played cricket in Newfoundland and accepted an invitation to join a team. When in his first game he made a hash of it, his excuse was that, "I don't know much about the way *you people* play it." If he didn't know much about cricket he soon learnt about English accents. When in 1998 I asked him why it was that he was one of very few people to return from a prolonged stay in England without an accent, he observed that since there were no fewer·than a dozen distinct accents just among the sixty boys at St. Chad's he wouldn't have known which one to choose. "Besides," he added, "I didn't want to come back stuck up." George had learned that 'dialects' exist only in the ears of people who speak another one. The lesson helps to explain why he felt so comfortable in using Change Islands dialect in his speeches and writing, and indeed in his private speech.

In a speech at Durham University marking St. Chad's Day in 1957, just before he left England for Queen's College, George recalled his student days, taking a swipe or two at the queer language spoken there and the ignorance Englishmen show of Newfoundland. The effusive introduction given him by the principal of St. Chad's gave him his opening lines. A famous speaker, he began, used to say that the three hardest things to do were to "climb a fence leaning towards you, kiss a girl leaning away from you and to acknowledge with proper humility a flattering introduction." Going on to pay tribute to St. Chad's on her special day, he recalled his stay there eighteen years before. "My own debt is rather unique in that this was my first home in England. When I came here I had neither friends nor countrymen though I thought I detected a few Romans" (a reference to the High Church element). In chastising the audience for their ignorance of their oldest colony he told of the "self-important vicar of a self-important parish" recently asking him whether Newfoundland had electricity; and of his reply, "I think it's in the air."

Neither in England nor at home was George ever hesitant to cut down anyone casting aspersions on his native land.

George had gone to England with the firm intention of returning to Newfoundland on getting his bachelor's degree from Durham in May 1940. But now, with Britain at war, the Expeditionary Force retreating to Dunkirk that very month, he decided to volunteer as chaplain in the armed forces. While awaiting his call-up he accepted the curacy of the new St. Peter's Church in Monkseaton, near Newcastle, where the rector, Father H.S.S. Jackson, emphasized the muscular Christianity George so much admired in his Uncle Tom Richards. He was welcomed to the church as "The Revd. G.H. Earle from Newfoundland," and would have wished for no higher commendation. (When the new church of St. Peter was dedicated in June 1938 its first curate, made deacon in the same month, was cruising on the *Argonaut* an ocean away.)

As it turned out he served that church throughout the war, with momentous consequences for his personal life and career. Both church and government had concluded after World War I that the absence from their parishes of so many clergymen had seriously weakened the fabric of society, and had decreed that henceforth in a crisis of that scale clergymen could join the armed forces only with permission of the bishop. The new Bishop, Noel Hudson, decided that Monkseaton was one of the parishes from which the curate could not be spared. Monkseaton (site of early monks) was a dormitory town for the adjacent industrial area of Newcastle ten or so miles to the south. Just inland from the excellent beaches on which a prong of a German landing was then expected, Monkseaton was in a strategic position and therefore needed all the defenses and manpower it could muster. Moreover it was in the target area for *Luftwaffe* raids on Newcastle, which began

Monkseaton, near Newcastle, England, 1941.

as early as August 1940. It was for these and other reasons that the Bishop wanted area churches fully manned.

George himself served in Air Raid Precautions throughout the war. Indeed he had taken training as a warden in September 1939 in Silksworth. While taking training in defence against the "awful stuff" that was mustard gas and lewisite, he described in graphic detail in a letter to his brother Fred the terrible effects these gasses had on the skin, but, being George, couldn't resist adding, "I wouldn't have minded in the least using gas on you when you used to put your cold feet on me." George kept a diary throughout the war years at Monkseaton. While daily summaries of war news make up perhaps ninety percent of it, there are many references to his work as air raid warden and curate, and revealing glimpses into his state of mind.

Partly because the new St. Peter's Church was just establishing such organizations as women's groups and the Anglican Young People's Association, and also because of wartime demands, including chaplaincy to the ARP and visiting bereaved families, the pace of George's work and the long hours pushed him to the brink of mental and physical exhaustion. On top of all he worked throughout on his M.A. thesis, for which he received the degree from Durham on July 11, 1944.

In the early years of the war numerous bombs intended for the industrial areas around Newcastle fell in George's neighbourhood. One, destroying an adjacent house—"a real racket"—falling on his very first night in Monkseaton, another damaging St. Peter's Church. The most extensive damage was incurred on the night of August 15, 1942 when a hundred bombers accompanied by forty fighters dropped explosive and incendiary bombs over a wide area. "This day," George noted, "will never be forgotten. I was in bed nearly asleep when I heard a plane flying over.... The scream of high explosives found me rolling myself in bedclothes and jumping. When I emerged the whole district was lit with incendiaries, one of which was under my bedroom window." On December 31, 1942 he wrote in his last entry for the year, "The war goes on and so do the years. 1942 has been one of ups and downs, internationally and personally.... May 1943 bring peace and happiness."

L to R: Ray Layman, George, brother Harry. Monkseaton.

Although George was a person of sanguine tempera-
ment, he was, then, under severe stress at Monkseaton,
especially in 1942 and 1943. But the many visits he received
from Newfoundland servicemen, most of them from
Change Islands and Fogo, brought him welcome diversions. The most frequent visitor was his brother Harry,
who was in the Royal Navy. Their wining and dining and
conversations that never ended before midnight usually
ended in happy recollections of boyhood in Change Islands. Sadly, on September 25, 1942 George received from
his father a telegram, "Harry reported missing from war-
ship *Zulu.*" That evening he wrote in his diary, "The
dreaded cable arrived today from Dad saying that Harry
has been reported missing from HMS *Zulu.* It's impossible
to express in words the feeling within — the sense of loss
and agony must be experienced to be grasped." On the
night of September 13/14 the *Zulu*, a light cruiser, had been
shelling enemy-held Tobruk and covering the landing
craft sent in to destroy ammunition dumps. Damaged, she

was bombed and sank en route to Alexandria the next afternoon.

Two months later, on November 11, George was happily able to record, "Of all news to receive on this day was a cable from Mother saying that Harry is a prisoner of war in Italian hands." On March 24, 1943 he received a telegram from Harry himself, "Repatriated. Fit and well. Hope to see you soon." It was June 24 before Harry showed up in Monkseaton. That night "we talked till 6 in the morning when I got up and went to church." The report from Harry was that when the landing craft ferrying commandos to Tobruk to blow up ammunition dumps was sunk, he, one of few survivors on the craft, swam ashore and after three hours' of fighting surrendered to the Italian garrison. (After leave in Fogo Harry returned to the navy and as asdic operator on a destroyer participated in the D-Day landing in Normandy. The war over, he made a successful career in engineering in England and later in Rhodesia.)

Another visitor who brought George great pleasure was Bernard Thomas Scammell of Change Islands, Arthur's brother, who was a bombardier in the Royal Air Force. From December 17, 1942 to May 12 of the next year Tom visited George five times. On one occasion while out for a walk they were caught in an air raid. Tom was "scared stiff." "Now," said George, "you can see what it's like down here — while you're up there plastering Germans." To which Tom agreed, "That's the difference — being on the receiving end." George's entry on Tom's first visit records, "Tom and I had a grand day.... We talked, sang, smoked, ate and reminisced about Old Change Islands Anecdotes." On May 14, 1943 George hailed the "grand news" that Tom, having flown thirty sorties over enemy territory, had been assigned to ground crew for six months' respite from flying. Sadly, a few weeks later Tom lost his life on an English airfield while trying to rescue crew from a burning aircraft. George recorded his grief in his July 21 entry. "A very great blow to me was news of Tom Scammell's death.... The fact that his death occurred as the result of an accident when we thought he was out of danger made it harder to believe and bear. May he rest in peace with God."

Scammell's death occasioned a poem in which, notwithstanding the last verse, George's faith in God and His ways is clearly stretched to the breaking point. Titled "Troubled," it was published in St. Peter's church magazine in July 1943.

> O God, I cannot see to-night.
> I'm looking by Thy grace to see,
> My eyes are dimmed with agony.
> O, lead me from Gethsemane.
> I cannot see to-night.
>
> O God, I cannot think to-night.
> I'm struggling by Thy grace to think,
> But I am trembling on the brink.
> O, of Thy cup of peace to drink!
> I cannot think to-night.
>
> O God, I cannot pray to-night.
> I'm aching by Thy grace to pray,
> But Oh! Thou art so far away;
> Why seemest Thou to answer nay?
> I cannot pray to-night.
>
> O God, I cannot sleep to-night.
> I'm fighting by Thy grace to sleep,
> But I can only sob and weep.
> Yes, I am crying from the deep.
> I cannot sleep to-night.

But God, I must not doubt to-night.
Thy Son hath calmed the troubled breast
And given to the weary rest.
I, waiting, cry, "Thy Will is best."
I **will** not doubt to-night.

Arthur Scammell's fine war poem "These Shall Not
Return" in memory of his brother Bernard Thomas, DFM
also bears mentioning here. Beautifully crafted, unfeigned
and deeply moving, it is a tribute not to one person but to
all the war dead. The first and fourth verses capture its
sentiment.

These shall not return.
Each in his hour on alien lands or seas,
They read Death's contract, gauged the sacrifice,
Then named their loved ones beneficiaries,
And freely paid the price.

These shall not return.
They would have died again to spare you this.
They may not come and sit and talk with you,
But in the silent places of the heart
They have home-comings too.

Eventful though the Monkseaton experiences were for
the young curate, the most far-reaching event was his
meeting the young woman with whom he would share a
rich life for more than half a century. The circumstances of
their meeting would have been unthinkable to Elna a
month before. When the rector of St. Peter's Church, Father H.S.S. Jackson, assigned his curate the task of forming
a local of the Anglican Young People's Association he gave
him a list of potential candidates that included Elna Smith-
Tennant. Elna would have been surprised to know that
she was even considered a potential member of the
staunchly Anglican A.Y.P.A., for she was neither an Angli-

can nor a churchgoer. Nonetheless after George contacted her through her elder sister Aileen, who attended St. Peter's church, she reluctantly agreed to attend the organizing meeting. In retrospect at least, it is clear that from their first meeting, on January 24, 1941, George saw in the intelligent, strong-willed and good-looking Elna potential beyond membership in the youth organization. His diary notes, "Elna attended for the first time tonight and so my first time meeting her. Somehow she seemed different from others." Five days after the January 24 meeting the dutiful curate wrote Elna reminding her of the responsibility she was taking on in joining the church youth organization and assuring her that, although membership was "generally reserved for confirmed members of the Church," chaplains of branches were "allowed to use their discretion." The letter added that, should you be experiencing difficulties with membership "I would gladly give you a visit and make things clear." This was the voice of a chaplain more than willing to use his discretion in this case.

Elna's church background was eclectic. When her paternal grandfather Smith, a Liverpool Quaker, married an Anglican he insisted that the ceremony take place in the Quaker Meeting House, and brought up his family of four, including Elna's father, in the Quaker faith. After grandfather Smith died at an early age, his widow married an Anglican, a Captain John Tennant, and Elna's father, a Smith-Tennant now, became an Anglican. (John Tennant, a sea captain, died in Montreal and is buried there.) Yet another turn was taken when Elna's father married her mother, a woman of stern Shetland Islands Presbyterian stock. Sadly, when Elna was only ten her mother Agnes (nee Williamson) at forty-seven died of a brain aneurism. Whereupon her father married another Presbyterian, her mother's cousin from the Shetland Islands. As is often the case with children of mixed-church homes, Elna grew up with an indifference to religion and hair-splitting church doctrines. Her religious state when George met her can best be described as dormant Presbyterian.

The first hint of courtship, or of the prelude to courtship, in George's diary appeared on April 19, 1941. "Went to the cinema in night with Elna Tennant and saw 'Foreign Correspondent.' Not bad — both picture and Elna." Thereafter there were increasing numbers of movies, walks in parks and open fields, and visits to historic sites. A May 24 "grand day" visiting the Venerable Bede's Church of St. Paul in Jarrow was marred only by the news of the sinking of HMS *Hood*, Britain's largest and fastest battleship, with the loss of all but three of her crew. In the first months of courtship the curate and ordained priest thought it prudent to restrict himself to what the famous Dorset dialect poet, William Barnes, called "A Bit of Sly Coortin." Thus on July 2 (1941) after Elna had attended a church meeting, "Elna was present but couldn't get the nerve for a walk — too many eager eyes to so break forth;" and on September 23, after an A.Y.P.A. meeting, "Elna was there but too many interested 'spies' to boldly accompany her home. Not all sunshine courting in a parish." But love finds her ways. Although an air raid alert was a summons to an ARP warden to hasten to his station, on the evening of October 3, 1941, with bombs falling in the Monkseaton area, George "made it part of my ARP duty to visit Elna during a raid." Caught walking with Elna in one air raid alert, George's chivalry was put to a severe test. As the sirens sounded he quickly put on his tin ARP helmet and turned to Elna, "I'm very sorry I don't have a helmet for you." Although this was a lapse in courtly manners that George was not allowed to forget and to which thereafter he was always ready to confess, the courtship, though shaky at times, was marked by progress.

Indeed by June of that year George was able to record, "Spent evening at my second home, Tennants." Elna, a secretary with Lucas engineering, which produced war matériel, was then living at home with her father, step-mother and her older sister Aileen. In his uncertainty about winning Elna's hand it must have seemed a step forward for the young colonial to be 'accepted' by a watch-ful father who in Elna's memory was "the last of the Victorians." Yet George had still a great obstacle to face. Even though Elna became a confirmed member of the church and a regular churchgoer she was still apprehen-sive about the vocation of a clergyman's wife. Nor was she reassured by George's somewhat ingenuous promise that he "didn't want to marry an assistant curate." Had this city girl been able to foresee her first year as vicar's wife in rural Falstone she probably would have been even more appre-hensive.

Meanwhile, at a Retreat for clergymen in an isolated fell of County Durham in June 1941 George, considering it not "at all irrelevant to use part of this time in deep thought with and about Elna," had put to himself the question, "celibacy or marriage to Elna?" For comfort, if not for complete assurance, he now invoked divine intervention. "I really believe God is guiding me to Elna and her to me. Our very meeting and all the circumstances point so clearly. May she see it too." His prayer — or more likely his persistence and charm — brought the desired outcome. Engaged in March 1944, the Anglican priest and former Presbyterian were married on November 12, 1945.

When in 1963 the Monkseaton church celebrated its silver anniversary its first curate, then Principal G.H. Earle of Queen's College, sent a greeting to its magazine. Al-though brief, it is a vivid recollection of life in the parish during the war years.

The Earle wedding party, 1945. L to R: Rev. Norman Southcott, Connie Hunter, Elna's sister Aileen, Rev. Oswald Dickenson.

Your church was two years old when I came to you as your first Curate in 1940. Just over a month later I witnessed the total destruction of the old tin church and the shaking of the new. The Vicar, Father Jackson, received a severe shock that night in body and soul; he would not talk much but I saw it and resolved to stay with him as long as possible.... The Vicar became my hero and still is, for death doth not divide us.... How he inspired me to read, pray, work and apply my Christian belief to daily living!

As I reminisce I see those war years in bold relief: crawling round the blacked-out parish during air raids, sneaking down into the stokehole when things got 'hot,' drinking cups of all sorts of stuff in the A.R.P. depot, not to mention the nightly round and uncommon task of trying to keep the parish intact. My pride and joy was the A.Y.P.A. which met through thick and thin.... My dearest memory, of course, is the Church where we worshipped together, with no windows to lighten our steps, but where the Light of the World truly shone. May God bless her now and in the future.

After eighteen years in your country I returned home to head my old College, but I did not leave you behind, for my better half is one of you. Elna joins me in sending greetings to all who remember us and those who know us not. God be with you.

Country Parson

George's last duty at Monkseaton was his 1945 Armistice Day sermon. Meanwhile he had been appointed rector of Falstone, Northumberland County, a village about forty miles northwest of Monkseaton. The Earles left for Falstone following their marriage the next day, detouring for a three-day honeymoon at the charming ivy-clad George Inn in the secluded hamlet of Chollerford (near Hexham). The privacy so much coveted by honeymooners was briefly threatened when on entering the dining room of their inn they were greeted by their wedding picture on the front page of the paper diners were reading. That little embarrassment passed, they enjoyed the three days, albeit under dark November skies, strolling along the South Tyne and visiting any historic sites the rural area offered.

Although Falstone itself is a small village, the parish, covering about a hundred square miles stretching northwestward to the Scottish border, was the largest in England. Set in the valley of the North Tyne, Falstone, itself pastoral, is surrounded by fells and tablelands broken only by dark volcanic peaks and by steep gorges through which small burns tumble into the Tyne. The character of the land is told in surrounding topographical names — Highfield Moor, White Hill, Earl's Seat, Jock's Pike, Copplestone Fell and Paddaburn Moor. On these treeless moors grow only bracken, coarse grass and heather, with here and there huddled patches of wild berries, including a few bakeap-

73

George Inn, Chollerford, near Hexham, scene of the Earles' honeymoon, November 1945.

ples. The tableland, often dark and foreboding under lowering cloud from the North Sea, is made even more barren by chilling rains and snow borne on the northeasterlies. It is on this stark and infertile land that sheep and cattle farmers, scattered through the narrow haughs or valley floors, have for a thousand years struggled to keep body and soul together. It was this stock, supplemented by families of young men reforesting nearby Kielder Forest, that constituted George's parish.

Local history was no less tortured than the volcanic tableland. A Belgium of battlefields, from the sixth century to the early eighteenth Northumberland had been invaded and ravaged by Angles, Britons and Vikings; and, later, in the Border wars between Scottish and English kings. As one historian put it, "The history of the North is essentially a drum and trumpet history." Over two hundred monuments dot the landscape, while hundreds of cairns mark the lonely places where men died. Not surprisingly this turbulent history has inspired a wealth of ballads, dirges and tales. Perhaps only in Scotland is history so deeply embedded in legend.

It is quite possible that had Earle settled permanently in urban Newcastle, Sunderland or even Monkseaton, instead of moving to the rural countryside of Northumberland, he would never have turned to the "old foolishness" of Newfoundland as a repository of our history. For, as he was to tell many Newfoundland audiences, it was in rural Northumberland, where legend was an oracle, that he learned that folklore far from being a leftover of history is the very embodiment of it. In notes probably made for his 1979 M.U.N. convocation speech he recalled, "I went to a sprawling parish in N.W. Northumberland, which adjoined Scotland. Here I saw simplicity again, the enjoyment of simple things, the round-the-clock work of the farmer, forester and shepherd, the humour which I compared with my native land. I became part of their life, learnt their folk songs, heard their folk stories and danced their folk dances. And I thought we have a blend in Newfoundland — English and Celtic." "And so," he told the M.U.N. convocation, "returning to Newfoundland after imbibing the folklore of Northern England I listened with more sensitive ears and looked with more attentive eyes...." In a word, he had come to see that folklore is the most perfect mirror of ordinary life.

The Earles arrived in Falstone by train on the afternoon of November 15, 1945. A tiny village of about two hundred people, Falstone was a little oasis in the bleak landscape consisting only of a few weathered cottages, a Presbyterian church and manse, a cobbler shop, a tailor shop, a smithy, two small general stores and the ubiquitous pub, the Black Cock; and of course the Anglican church and rectory. A visitor to the North Tyne a few months before George was born singled out Falstone for its natural beauty and charm. "Set amongst trees, in the midst of pleasant meadows, it is a welcome relief from the bare fells and moorlands around it." It hadn't changed in the intervening thirty years, nor in the last hundred. Writing in the parish bulletin in 1970, George's successor, the Reverend Francis Eddershaw, captures the unchanging scene of "great natural beauty . . . the breathtaking loveliness of a crisp winter morning, the sounds of the curlew and snipe and cuckoo in early autumn, and the rich colours of bracken and tree in the autumn."

The rectory to which George took his urban bride was the most imposing structure in the village. Built about 1820, the 16-room mansion was set at the back of a spacious meadow stretching from wooded slopes behind it to the Tyne River in front. A tourist driving along the narrow road that leads on to the Scottish border would have supposed that he was looking at a fine mansion where the Squire and his family lived in grace and comfort. But he would have been mistaken. Last occupied by an elderly couple, and before that used now and then by absentee incumbents, the house was badly run down and, without electricity, lacked all "modern conveniences." There were few curtains and new furniture for one bedroom. Even if money had been available, under the severe war-related shortages and rationing there were no such domestic items to buy. Lighted by kerosene lamps, one of them the touchy Aladdin, the virtual ice-box was "heated" mainly by a tiny stove in the spacious kitchen. There were several fireplaces upstairs and down, but with coal severely rationed most of them were unused. Thus several of the sixteen rooms had to be closed off and were never re-opened in the Earles' time. "M-y-y son!," George recalled in 1998, "we used to bivver with the cold, the like never felt in Change Islands." The second winter, 1946-47, was the coldest and stormiest winter in North England in more than fifty years. The most homey presence in the rambling house was Misty the cocker spaniel puppy given to the Earles as a wedding present.

Elna's domestic skills were severely tested in regulating lamp wicks, cleaning the globes or preventing them from getting smoked up in the first place, and in keeping the sluggish fireplaces burning. The Aladdin lamp defied her understanding as George found on arriving home one late afternoon to a smoke-filled room. "How stunned can you be," George quipped in the presence of a silent Elna, "to screw down an Aladdin — everybody knows that they smoke if you turn them down." Yes, everybody with Change Islands experience or a degree in thermodynamics.

Washing clothes was another challenge. After the custom of the area, washing consisted of boiling the clothes in a brick vat built over a fireplace in the scullery. The clothes were dried by running them through a mangle or hand-roller. To the chagrin of a woman anxious to make a good impression on her rural neighbours, Elna in dry seasons was obliged to hang out brownish clothes from the gravity-fed peaty water from their well on the hillside. (George, no stranger to water buckets, fetched drinking water from a well at the foot of their meadow.) The clothes were ironed by a flatiron heated by filling its cavity with red-hot bolts from the fireplace. Elna considered it a big advance when her father gave her a gas iron. The only problem was that, like the Aladdin lamp, it was erratic, now and then ejecting plumes of fire from its back end. While in her first winter in Falstone Elna was struggling with these new domestic problems and her duties as "assistant curate," she was expecting her first child, Christine, born in November 1946.

While Elna was turning the inhospitable old mansion into a home, George of course was doing his daily rounds in the parish. He had been appointed to the living of

Falstone by the Bishop of Newcastle. A living in old English churches is the arrangement whereby the incumbent
was paid not by the local or national church, but from
mostly ancient endowments, such as Queen Anne's
Bounty of 1704, established for the purpose; or by the lord
of the manor who 'owned' the church. In the case of
Falstone the living, in the parlance of the time, was "in the
gift of" the Lords of Admiralty. Generally, these gifts were
not intended to be the sole stipend, but to supplement
other assumed income. Up to the time of George's appointment in 1945 Falstone, for instance, had been a living
for retired naval chaplains with pensions, and in most
cases with private income.

One consequence of this 'living' arrangement was that
the stipends varied from parish to parish by as much as
thousands of pounds. The Falstone living of £270 a year
didn't go down well with the first non-naval incumbent,
who, after serving as a locum for the rector at Easington for
two weeks, wrote his brother Fred in March 1940, "The
rector gets about £1800 and isn't on the dole." Another
practical if not logical consequence of livings was that by
ancient custom local churches took no responsibility for
the maintenance of rectories or the rector's travel expenses. This put George, the first rector without a private
income, in a financial bind. And to complicate Elna's
household management, the Admiralty pay came only
every three months. Household managers will understand Elna's recalling, "Every third month was very tight."
On February 13 of their first winter in Falstone, the Bishop
of Newcastle wrote "My dear Earle" expressing understanding of the "hard work" to be done there. "You are
often in my thoughts, and I am writing to ask you how you
and your good wife are prospering in the work.... I gather
that things financial are not too easy, so I am sending
herewith a cheque for £10, which I hope may be of some

George's church, Falstone, Northumberland.

help." (After the war the church rationalized the financial chaos, and now sets a minimum stipend for parish priests.)

St. Peter's was the only Anglican church serving an area of a hundred square miles. Situated in the North Tyne valley, it is nestled among stately trees, some dwarfing its Norman tower, and is backed by a gentle slope that becomes treeless as it ascends to imposing fells. A worthy subject for the postcards which featured it, by contrast it must often have reminded its new rector of the bleak setting of St. Margaret's church in Change Islands. About all that reminded him of his home church were the dim gas lamps flickering against the darkness. When on his first Saturday in the parish George, preparing for Sunday services, asked the warden about the size of Sunday congregations, he was told "Fair to middlin'," and could elicit no more precise answer. As it turned out, the average congregation was ten people; only on special occasions would as many as twenty show up. "Double digits," George recalled, "that was ok — I always did the full service no matter how small the congregation." The 'Methodist' idea

of packing churches, "compelling them to come in," had
become foreign to Falstone, as it was to most English
churches. The focus of the Anglican church was sacra-
ments, not public worship as such. And it was for this
reason that not only for Anglicans but for nonconformists
"the church," i.e. the Anglican Church as distinct from
chapel and kirk, retained its historic place in English vil-
lages and certainly in Falstone.

Partly from necessity, therefore, and also inspired by
the practical Christianity of Uncle Tom Richards, George
took his ministry directly to the people, regularly visiting
farmers, needy people and the sick, and even holding
services for a handful of neighbours in scattered farm
houses and in the remote hunting castle of the Duke of
Northumberland; and serving on such community bodies
as the electricity board through which he helped to get
"the electric" in the Falstone area in 1952, the year he left.
For the first three years, unable to buy a car on his Admiralty living and without a local travel allowance, the penu-
rious rector bicycled the ten miles of the Tyne Valley road
almost to the Scottish border, with detours up the steep
haughs to remote farmsteads. The hilly country not only
taxed his physical energy, but after dark the narrow, lonely
haughs or gorges peopled with as many ghosts as farmers
were as nerve-wracking as the haunted road from Seldom
to Fogo in his courting days. It was not only to light Elna's
lamps that he always tried to scurry home before dark.

It was on his daily rounds that George met characters
no less colourful than Change Islands' Skipper John Chaffey and old Jacob Steele, uncle Bob Hawkins and old Billy
Cave. As many of them, especially the old men, fancied
themselves philosophers and theologians, the rector "had
to be on guard all the time — to be stumped was to lose
face." One old codger, known as "Bob the philosopher,"
was always lying in wait for George, "a real torment, he

was." When George dropped in to see him after his octogenarian mother died at home, he was challenged: "I decided to test this business of a soul leaving the body at death. So when she was dying I closed every door and window a soul could escape through and fly off and be immortal. There was no evidence of a soul in the locked-up room." Pausing to light his pipe, he sprung the question, "Now, how can you explain that?" Knowing that his answer had to be immediate and convincing, George shot back a question, "Did you close off the fireplace?" "My God," old Bob confessed, "that's the one escape I forgot to close." "Well there you are!," replied a smug rector. Not all of the rector's theological answers gave him such satisfaction. George was more at home with the parishioner who in telling neighbours of a visit from him reported, "We had the rector in. I enjoyed his visit —there was no religion about him."

Some of the questions George got in this isolated region of the North were about Newfoundland. These the ardent expatriate was always glad to answer. Stunned questions, however, not only offended him, but could trigger his sometimes quick temper. One dear old lady never missed an opportunity to ask about Newfoundland, "does the snow ever melt, how cold are igloos in winter and do they leak, can you put the electric in igloos?" One day her theme was whales, their size in particular fascinating her. "Yes," replied George, "they can grow up to hundreds of feet long. But in Newfoundland we have a fish that can swallow one of them." "Dearie me! I never heard of that before. Amazing. What is the name of the fish?" "A sculpin," said George. "Well, well, how interesting — I shall have to go and read up." Thereafter, her faith in her rector shaken, she refrained from asking more questions.

The gravedigger in Falstone, like his brothers the world over, was as remarkable for his commitment to the trade as for his expertise. While he was paid a pound per grave, it was not money that sustained his enthusiasm. As he told Rector Earle, "I love the work and always look forward to it. There's nothing I'd rather be doing." But keen though he was, he didn't quite match the initiative of his counterpart in George's next parish in Choppington. Always on the look-out for failing health, especially among elderly parishioners, he reported regularly to his partner the rector, who, like himself, received a pound per funeral. One evening he came to the back door of the rectory bursting with first-hand knowledge of his elderly land-lady, "She's coughing a lot and fast losing weight. Rector, I think she'll soon be ours." Later in telling these stories in Newfoundland Canon Earle was making a case for more humour in the church.

Perhaps the most memorable character the Earles en-countered was Albert the tramp. He was one of that proud band of professional tramps who, with their worldly goods tied to a bicycle or pushed in a cart, plied the country roads of north England and Wales from spring to autumn right up to the 1970s. So much of an institution had the tramping fraternity become that there were standard signs, à la B&B signs, for display by homes ready to wel-come them for a meal or a night or two. One spring day Albert turned up at the rectory. Born in the slums of Newcastle, he told George that he had been such a cross baby that he had to be fed gin with his milk. In the winters he always managed to find a jail to stay in, preferably a Scottish one "because they have carpeted floors and are more comfortable than the English." Given accommoda-tion in the rectory's hay loft and provided with whatever meals his hosts enjoyed, Albert wore out his welcome by staying for a month. One step the Earles took to get rid of him was to cut down on the quantity and quality of his meals. It worked. His sense of pride and dignity offended, Albert, accusing his hosts of "class distinction," left in a huff. In notes made later on Albert's stay, George observed that it was time for him to leave because he had become "a bit familiar" and "was beginning to steal a bit."

The best place to meet a cross section of English villagers is at the local pub. For that reason, and no doubt for others, George considered it his bounden duty to drop in now and then. While having a pint on the house or on a generous parishioner he could hear about farmers' latest woes, about sick people, rogues and adulterers, about government waste and the good old days. The pub was the Change Islands twine loft. On his first visit to the Black Cock George heard a tale of a different kind. The publican, having confirmed that the new rector was indeed a Newfoundlander, complained how on every Saturday night during the war Newfoundlanders in a forestry unit at nearby Kielder Forest "used to come in and after a few shots of rum bought by the bottle wreck the bar." Pub wreckers or Pentecostals, George could brook no criticism of his fellow countrymen. "They wouldn't have wrecked your pub if you hadn't sold them rum by the bottle."

Soon after George settled in Falstone he began to harbour thoughts of treating his well-indoctrinated bride to a visit back to the Isles of the Blest where sun rays crown the stately pine and ponies graze the smiling land, where godly Anglicans pack the capacious church of St. Margaret, where men tell tales of bravery, and wits their taller tales. By the spring of 1948 he felt the time had come. But with a daughter only a year and a half old and with saving to buy a car, it was decided that George should visit Newfoundland alone. And so it was that, at the very time when the frenzy of the Berlin blockade seemed to be heralding a third world war, in June George embarked on

R.M.S. *Nova Scotia* in Liverpool for St. John's. Of the war threat George later quipped that wars always seemed to be started around him: the first war when he was born, the second just as he arrived for a year's study in England, the likely third, as it then seemed to many observers, getting under way in the skies over Berlin.

On the eve of his departure from Falstone George received a (June 6) letter from his father wishing him "a pleasant trip across the Herring Pond" and making an extraordinary request. "If you happen to be passing any pawnshops and they have any fairly good watches to sell fairly cheap, you might get one and bring out to me.... Some of the Forestry men brought out some they got in a pawnshop." George's dollar-conscious father added the caution, "If you have to pay duty, should you get one, don't value it too high." Perhaps while you are in St. John's, the letter added, you can get an idea of the freight charges to England as "I have a few tins of lobster and salmon to give you." There is no record of George's finding a watch, but he did return to England laden down with home produce ranging from bakeapples to salt cod — and another customs problem. With some basic foods rationed in England and others in short supply, George was delighted with the wide choices on the *Nova Scotia*'s menu. Challenged by the steward, at lunch one day he went through all three main courses, fish, steaks and cold plate, not missing the Scotch broth or the rice pudding, or the cheese, biscuits and coffee. On a copy of the menu for that day (July 10) is scribbled, "This is to certify that Rev. Earle went through the whole menu. D. Laundry, Table Mate."

George's summer visit to his parents in Fogo and to his scattered family, his return to the Change Islands of happy memory and the smells and sounds of the sea brought him the pleasures of an exile come home. He was disappointed, however, that the frenzied preoccupation of his old friends with the second referendum on the future form of government all but ruled out the kitchen banter he so fondly remembered. With the vote scheduled for July 22, old codgers and former schoolmates alike, their ears tuned to battery radios for the harangue of Joey Smallwood and Peter Cashin, wanted to talk about nothing else. As George recalled in a 1983 conversation with Malcolm MacLeod, "it was Joey bawling down Peter Cashin and he bawling down somebody else and pro and con, well how excited they got over it." A worse commotion than runnin' down Squires on the squid-jiggin' ground. "Just came home for a holiday and expecting all my friends to be pleased to see me and all that, and they all huddled up in the corner listening to the radio." Moreover the prospect of New-foundland's becoming a Canadian province had no more appeal to him than to his father. Although George became a Canadian citizen after his permanent return home in 1957, he never became Canadian at heart.

On that July visit George was blessed with one auspicious encounter. At an afternoon tea he met Otto Tucker, Salvation Army officer/teacher in Change Islands the year before. The immediate rapport between the Anglican priest and the Army officer later blossomed into one of the two or three warmest friendships of George's life. After they returned home they not only met frequently, but, although living in the same city, exchanged letters, most of them digging at each other. In a letter of July 22, 1990 George reminded his friend that it was "farty-two years ago I met you in the home of Mrs. Carrie Roberts...and conversed with you over tea and buns laced with jam.... I smoked, you didn't. I often think of that meeting in Change Islands in 1948 — providential." The letter ended, "You were the first — and last — foolish Salvation Army officer I ever met because on Change Islands I was not allowed to take part in wrong forms of worship."

In late July George returned to a rationed England weighed down with cartons of canned salmon, mussels, lobster and turr from his parents' production line, and with a trunk laden with gifts for Elna, clothing and toys for daughter Christine and a mountain of cigarettes from relatives and friends. He knew before his ship left St. John's that he had far more cigarettes than the English customs would allow duty free. No keener to pay duty on cigarettes than his father was to pay on pawned watches, he therefore stepped up his already heavy smoking. Still he had cartons left. When on his last night at sea it dawned on him that, in addition to cigarettes, customs also permitted entry of a pound of tobacco duty free, he broke up hundreds of cigarettes and bagged the tobacco separately. As for the other bounty, a customs man, struggling to lift it and muttering how clergymen could always be counted on to travel with a load of heavy books, quickly disposed of it with a clearance tag. It was a relieved man of the cloth who caught the train for Falstone.

As summer was a slow time in the parish, on returning home in August George could spend some time in the extensive vegetable garden he had cultivated to supplement his Admiralty income. Eschewing "fancy stuff" like broccoli or Brussels sprouts, he grew only the boyhood crops of beet, cabbage, carrot, turnip and potatoes. His one crop not found in Change Islands was tobacco, perhaps the most profitable of all. George carefully calculated his projected savings on the back of the instruction sheet for growing tobacco plants. At 20 cigarettes a day the annual saving would be about £63. "120 plants should produce 22½ pounds of tobacco = 360 ozs. or nearly an oz. a day for a year." Checked, his figures worked out — except for the estimate of 20 cigarettes a day. The gardener also kept hens, a couple of geese and one year a pig. He gave a colourful account of his farming in a letter to his parents in

December 1949. "Dad asked about the garden etc. Things turned out very well and I still have dozens of frost-resisting cabbage in the ground.... My hens have moulted and have started to lay for the winter. I sell as many eggs as I can to buy meal etc. I make the blighters pay for themselves and give me a little profit. Have two geese which I hatched in May and trying to get a gander to go with them."

While George's Falstone neighbours viewed his "firkin around" in the garden with interest, he also gained a bit of a reputation as a water diviner. Indeed he possessed the skill in a high degree, the divining rod, usually a birch or willow fork, invariably jerking earthward when he approached subterranean water. On one or two occasions the Northumberland Forestry Commission sought his help in finding water, and after he returned to Newfoundland he divined two or three wells around Conception Bay. But few of his friends and acquaintances ever knew that he was possessed of the gift. One would have thought that divining was an apt reference for a clergyman's after-dinner speeches, but curiously it appears that he never once mentioned it. While George gave many addresses in England, most on religion and several on Newfoundland, his only after-dinner, humorous speeches were given at two Burns Nights dinners at the Black Cock pub in Falstone. At one dinner he presented a take-off, "To a Rat," on Burns's "To a Mouse." Not up to his later standards, the poem is the first example of George's use of doggerel in humorous speeches. The first two verses read:

> Thou ugly, hairy loathesome creature
> The pest of farmer and of preacher
> Full I've set a poison trap
>   To stop thy breath.

But thou as e'er with wily measure
Refuse to take it as a treasure
But lay beside it for a nap
   Defying death.

George's only other humorous performances in Falstone were the skits he and his close friend Hamish Fairlie,
the Presbyterian minister, staged as fund-raisers for local
charities. Their most successful performance was a spoof
of the ingrained conservative outlook and habits of the
villagers. There was old Bill who daily whipped the pol-
luted waters of the Tyne because they were full of salmon
when he was a boy. For their frequent shopping in nearby
Bellingham villagers always took "the 8:10" although that
train schedule had been changed from 8:10 to 9:30 for a
generation. This inspired a skit "Bellingham Shopping."
Like most rural people, George's parishioners resisted all
change. When he tried to change times of church services
or meetings set a hundred years ago in different circumstances, he faced an outcry: "We've always met at these
times," "The new time is when I read my newspaper,"
"That change would interfere with milking time." This
resistance to change not only exasperated the rector, but
inspired another skit. To their credit, on viewing themselves in the mirror of satire the villagers laughed heartily.
If parishioners had any question, it was about their rector's
close association with a Presbyterian minister.

After George and Elna visited Falstone in 1973 with
Hamish and Ruth Fairlie, who had been their best friends
in the parish, George reflected, "One thing is sure — we
gave them fun in our day. Ours was the golden age
according to locals." On this May visit the villagers held a
reunion in the Black Cock to meet and treat their guests.
"What a day! Oh the mystery of memory. After over 20
years we visited together friends of old — Presbyterians

and Anglicans." One old character at the pub reminded George that he had once said of the tissue-thin Hexham newspaper, "It's the paper you read as you look through it." The skits were reviewed, and the Burns Nights, marriages and deaths and of course the challenging times for the churches in the aftermath of the war.

The Earles had spent six memorable years in Falstone. The Change Islander had found in the rustic kitchens and pub the twine-loft banter of his boyhood, had participated in village activities, including the Folk Dance Society, and had exceeded his bishop's expectations for "hard work" in a difficult parish. And he had been blessed with a family, Christine born in 1946 and Alison in 1950. But now, in February 1952, it was time to say goodbye. The day before he was inducted into his new parish in the coal mining, dusty town of Choppington he was moved to express in a poem, "On Leaving the Country," his feelings on leaving pastoral Falstone.

> The beauties of nature so long did surround me,
> The heather and hills, the silence around me,
> The songs of the birds, the cut of the plough,
> The call of the rooster — it's all ending now.
>
> The eyesores of man will soon, friend, surround me,
> The pit-heaps and engines will soon be around me,
> The clatter of buses, the screeching of brakes,
> The sirens and whistles and all that man makes.
>
> But what does it matter? It's people that count,
> Their spirit and nature, not heather and mount.
> In the midst of God's beauties there lurk ugly hearts,
> In most of man's eyesores are God's counterparts.

I'm not going for ease as one running from troubles,
Most grandiose schemes made by man are as bubbles.
I leave you my friends surrounded with beauty,
To face the unknown on a clear path of duty.

The Fighting Vicar

The Earles moved to Choppington, about thirty-five miles eastward, in the cold month of February 1952, when parishioners were in mourning for the February 6 death of George VI. In contrast with pastoral Falstone with its scattered five hundred people, Choppington was a bustling mining town of 9,000 surrounded by more collieries than farms. Since his appointment in the autumn George had been looking forward to the new challenge of the less idyllic parish because, as he told the North Tyne church magazine, he saw a greater scope for service in a large, more complex community, and because, as he told me, he was anxious to gain as wide an experience as possible before returning to Newfoundland.

George was inducted vicar of St. Paul's Church, Choppington, on February 18, 1952 by Bishop Noel Hudson of Newcastle, his bishop during the war years at Monkseaton. In commending him to the parish, the bishop observed that he was a Newfoundlander and a man of "singular wisdom and intelligence." At a reception following the induction, the new vicar was interviewed by the *News Post*, a regional newspaper. "Mr. Earle said that he had no interest in politics...enjoyed country dancing and American square dancing...and not until he knows Choppington's needs could he formulate a plan of action." From the Earles' personal point of view, the most vexatious fact the newspaper mentioned was that pending repairs to the

George's only attempt at pram pushing, Choppington, Peter apprehensive.

vicarage they would "live with Mrs. R. Miller, Windsor House, Guide Post."

George's introduction to Choppington was not auspicious. If the Falstone rectory had been inhospitable the 1868 Choppington vicarage, "a huge monstrosity" unoccupied for a year, was virtually uninhabitable. Its foundation having been weakened when coal shafts were dug too near it, the walls had gaping fissures and the roof was leaking. Yet the parish had supposed that the Earles would move in while the dilapidated house was being repaired. This George refused to do, arguing that it would be cheaper to build a new rectory and believing that in any case repairs would be drawn out and inadequate. When the newspaper reported that the Earles would live elsewhere until repairs were completed on the vicarage, it knew nothing of the new vicar's resolve to build a new vicarage. But within weeks it announced, "Choppington Vicarage, which is in a dilapidated condition and considered dangerous, is to be demolished, and on the adjacent lawn a new Vicarage costing £4,500 is to be erected in the very near future."

The next year, the dispute happily settled, George saluted the old vicarage in the church magazine. The sixty-line "Ode to the Old Vicarage" reads in part:

> The Vicarage looked through the trees
> And trembled somewhat at the knees
> And sighed, as humans sigh, and said
> "When we get old men wish us dead."
> With nasty twists at every door,
> (Her back had broken long before),
> Her slates tried hard to check the rain
> But tried, as humans try, in vain.
>
> But Vicarage, dry up your tears!
> You housed six Vicars o'er the years
> And those who shivered in your halls
> Oft leaned in laughter by your walls.
> You once were bonny, young and gay
> But now you go the self-same way
> As humans go when past their best
> And win some kind of endless rest.

Meanwhile, in the winter of 1952, the rectory "not fit to live in," the Earles lived in a self-contained unit of a private home. This was not only inadequate for a family of two children, but the home-owner was extremely fastidious, always running, for example, to sweep from the highly groomed walk-ways any mud or dead leaves from the children's shoes. This was an intolerable situation for a young mother of two active young children. On his daily rounds George therefore began to look for more suitable accommodations. Arriving home in his little 1930 Wolsey car one day he proudly announced, "I found a nice, spacious cottage, 'Willow Bridge.' It's available right away."

In Elna's questioning poor George about the cottage it was discovered that the charmingly named cottage, located on the edge of town, had no electricity. Of what use now the electric iron and "standard lamp" the Falstone parish had given Elna? Taken aback, George rushed off to see what the Electricity Board could do. When the manager agreed to run a light wire to the cottage, "just heavy enough to light a bulb or two and to run small appliances," one at a time, the Earles in desperation took the cottage.

Recalling the upheaval in 1998 George admitted, "It was the very worst house in Choppington, an old scrawley place." The Earles lived "on the wrong side of the tracks" for a full year, and it was there that their third child Peter was born in 1952. "M-y-y Son! What a place, a maze of a place — nothing in Change Islands as bad." In a warm letter of thanks to the parish on his leaving in 1957 George recalled, "Our early days were terribly inconvenienced domestically and we were not at peace. Few will realize how much we hated the first year and a half. Our efforts to provide a new home for present and future priests were met often with unworthy comments and false interpretation." The new rectory was blessed by the bishop on the evening of Friday, July 3, 1953. For the first time in their married lives the Earles were now living in comfort with "stoves, clothes-washers, electric radios and all that modern stuff." Moreover George's stipend was now £400 compared with Falstone's £270, and he was the first Choppington vicar to receive a car allowance.

The move to the new vicarage brought the Earles the domestic serenity they had missed for over a year. Except for one hair-raising night. While George was out that evening the dog brought Elna's attention to the warming oven on the Aga stove, where she found their cat Beauty apparently already suffocated. When George returned a little later he made a quick diagnosis and instituted revival operations. A dozen calls of "Here puss, come pussy, puss, puss, puss, here Beauty" and vigorous stroking brought no response. Later when light breathing was detected, or imagined, George agreed to stay up until a verdict could be rendered one way or another. Alone in the living room chain-smoking, the cat at his feet, he kept vigil for two hours. At midnight, Beauty's breathing now more pronounced, there came from outside a loud ethereal meow. Whereupon Beauty, uttering one sharp meow, shot three feet into the air, and fell to the carpet — dead.

Not surprisingly George was shaken by this turn of events. As the question *What in the world was that?* seized his mind, the man who had dodged ghosts on a lonely Fogo road and who had felt it prudent to pedal fast down the haunted fells of the Tyne was pretty sure that he knew the answer. He first told me the strange story of Beauty in 1988. Unnerved by it, I wrote him for minor clarifications. His reply a few days later seemed, wrongly, to assume that I was experiencing twinges of unbelief. "That story about the cat in the warming oven," he wrote, "was true. Remember our vicarage was surrounded on three sides by a cemetery or churchyard and on the fourth side had a

The haunted Choppington vicarage.

hawthorn hedge through which it was impossible to escape. Departed cats call to their loved ones too, you know."

Following Beauty's strange demise George began his "Ode to Beauty."

> A sympathetic, shrill, inviting meow
> Disturbed uncannily the midnight air
> As Beauty, victim of an accident
> Lay dying where so oft she lay asleep.
> The meow without the house, that single meow
> Reached its intended spot and instantly
> The semi-lifeless form meowed in reply
> And fell upon her pillow — still and dead.

In an unfinished second verse, he poses the question.

> I do not understand the ways of cats
> Now homely, now so far away
> What was that feline call so timely given?

Cast in the form of a ghost story, the account of Beauty's freakish death conceals the trauma George experienced. He enjoyed an extraordinary affinity with a succession of sixteen pets from their cocker spaniel in Falstone to the Siamese cat Ghengis the family had for thirteen years in St. John's. In addition to the notes on Beauty, George wrote up the loss of two other pets. When the cocker spaniel became possessive of George, sometimes snarling at Elna when she tried to pick up an item of George's clothes and baring her teeth at toddler Christine, the family gave her to a farmer as a gundog. "I'll never forget her last look. Feel it sorely," George recorded. "For the first time in my life I know by experience the love and faithfulness of a dog to her master and the pain the master feels when the parting comes. I only hope she's not suffering in heart as I am." George also left a detailed account of the death of another dog Impy, killed by a car near Queen's College on October 11, 1975. "The car ran over her with both wheels but somehow she got to me, got on my knee and looked and whimpered in a way I'll never forget. I laid her down and she died. I later buried her just outside our kitchen window at Queen's College." These notes were probably written for the book George had long intended to write on the family pets.

Inconvenienced though George's domestic life was for a year, as vicar he faced an even worse problem. Sited over the same coal tunnels that had undermined the rectory, the church had also suffered extensive damage from the sinking of its foundation. Repairs, if they could be effected at all, would cost more money than the parish could even contemplate raising. Told by parishioners that coal mining had caused the damage, the easygoing vicar now took on the bureaucratic National Coal Board in London, demanding full cost of repairs and restoration. Soon, not only local papers but one or two national publications were carrying headlines, "Vicar Fights Coal Board," "Vicar Takes on National Coal Board." After a prolonged fight the Coal Board not only agreed to pay for church restoration, but underwrote most of the cost of the new rectory. A great victory for the Change Islands colonial.

Meanwhile George's muse again took over, his "Choppington Parish Church 1866-1953" appearing in the November 1953 church magazine. The first two of four verses read:

> I started off most promising in eighteen sixty-six —
> The best of stone and furnishings, the best of lime and bricks;
> I had the best of everything that Choppington could give,
> And those who planned and founded me determined I should live.
> From century to century as other churches do
> To bear my witness, stand for truth and evil to eschew;
> And at my consecration by the Bishop of Dunelm
> I held my own in steadfastness with any in the realm.
>
> But now at eighty-seven years I'm broken and forlorn
> (I'm glad no one is left on earth who saw me newly-born);
> Some humans got in under me and hollowed out my bed
> (I did not ask to be interred for I was far from dead).
> I have a sinking feeling that beneath me is a hole
> Which should instead be solid rock and Choppington's Best Coal.
> With ceilings cracked and walls askew and floors all off the level
> I'm like the men of long ago possessed of every devil.

While George's efforts to restore St. Paul's Church building were crowned with almost miraculous success, his attempts to get parishioners to attend it were not. It remained difficult for one who had seen the Change Island church and other Newfoundland churches filled on Sundays to accept the fact that in England attendance of the vast majority was restricted to funerals, weddings and special occasions such as the June 1953 service to mark the Coronation of Elizabeth II. George's concern about the poor attendance was reflected in the remark he made later about his first service in Choppington. "When only twenty souls turned up I knew that there were 9000 still in bed." In a church magazine letter to parishioners in the first months of his incumbency the vicar made one of several pleas for greater participation in church services, "We apply ourselves to the task of building and extending Christ's Kingdom of love and prayer, of repentance and faith. I can still think of no better way of doing this than that which has worked so well elsewhere and could work here, namely to resolve to strengthen our Parish Communion by attending it every Sunday as a Christian family." The plea fell on deaf ears.

In Choppington as in Falstone and elsewhere women, mainly through The Mothers' Union, took on much of the practical work of the parish, their worldly reward an outing or two and a few games of cards at the vicarage. George was moved to give rhyme to one such outing, "The Mothers' Union Trip," a few lines of which follow.

> The last day of August, the morning was fine —
> We set off with gusto at quarter past nine;
> The bus headed westward, the party reclined
> So happy with duties at home far behind.
>
> The luxury bus sped us swift on our way
> To Morpeth and Whalton and on to Belsay,
> Through village and hamlet, past farmstead and
>   gorge
> And halted for coffee at Chollerford's "George."

The stop at the "George" in Chollerford was no doubt contrived by George and Elna as a return to their honeymoon inn. After thirty-six more lines recounting a stop at Hadrian's Wall and a longer visit to Carlisle, where "for three solid hours it rained and it rained/For three solid hours our patience was strained," the party set out for home.

> We twisted through by-roads and bended at bends
> And climbed sides of mountains like Everest friends
> We sang and made faces and laughed nearly sore
> Till nine o'clock found us at Choppington's door.

In one number of the parish magazine the poetic vicar promoted a Mothers' Union jumble sale.

> If little Willie's coat is tight,
> Or Mary's frock too small,
> With baby's shoes and father's hat
> Just place them on the Stall.
>
> From children's toys to Granny's socks,
> From ornaments to shoes;
> They, when assembled in the Hall,
> Make headline Jumble news.
>
> Out with unwanted pots and pans
> And garments large or small
> Be drastic with your souvenirs
> And send them to the Hall.

In the course of my dozen or so 'structured' interviews with George in 1998 and 1999 he would often mention that he had a clipping, a poem or photographs about the matter under discussion, but usually forgot to search for them. Next to Monkseaton, the best documented period was the Choppington years, from which several documents have already been quoted. In November 1998 he wrote me, "I've been firking around my files and I've surprised myself how much I've kept." While at Choppington the family took several holidays in their caravan (RV) near beaches on the North Sea. Four or five of these outings were recorded in rhyme. In his lengthy "A Caravan Holiday" George writes as a family man.

> You bring your water from a tap
> And put your rubbish in a hole;
> You learn to be a tidy chap
> And rest your body, mind and soul.
>
> With wife and children you are one
> Within the confines of a 'van';
> You share each other's work and fun
> And vie to get the darkest tan.
>
> And then it's past, a pleasant dream
> As to an end all things come;
> Refreshed you travel as a team
> And say you're thankful to be home.

In "Holiday Time," published in the church magazine, it is the parish priest who speaks. After references to "caravan and sands" and spending money with no thought for the morrow, the poem ends:

> So, what once were holy days
> Now have taken on new ways.
> Modern folk go far and fast
> While prosperity may last.
> Some, however, cannot go —
> Sick and poor and old and slow —
> May they in a peaceful way
> Find with God their holiday.

Despite the numerous poems George wrote, beginning with his Queen's College days in 1936 and 1937, he

L to R: George, Alison, Peter, George's mother, Christine, Elna, Choppington, England 1956.

never imagined himself a poet. Indeed some of his doggerel is in first draft, while few poems went beyond a
second. His aim in taking to rhyme was simply to record
events, to poke fun at human foibles, including his own, or
to play with and record the rich Newfoundland dialect.
Nevertheless he had a way with words, and the turning of
a phrase, like his quick wit, was a natural gift.

From the time George went to England in 1939 he had
nurtured the idea of one day returning 'home.' In Christmas week 1955 when on the BBC he heard of Bishop
Abraham's death a day or two before, George's mind was
flooded with memories of his 1938 trip on the *Argonaut* as
the Bishop's chaplain, and at the same time was "immediately seized with the idea that my own future was tied up
with the death of Abraham." When it seemed clear that
Canon J.A. Meaden, Principal of Queen's College, would
succeed Bishop Abraham, George wrote him expressing
interest in the principalship of Queen's. In reply Meaden
agreed that the principalship "would be an interesting
position." A subsequent letter from Meaden, who was
then administering the diocese, assured George that an
application from him would be "favourably received."
After his election as bishop in May 1956, Meaden wrote on
behalf of Queen's Corporation offering George the
Queen's position. Vicar Earle announced his retirement
from the Choppington parish in December 1956.

His incumbency at Choppington had been crowned
with brilliant success, not only in restoring the church and
building a new vicarage largely at the Coal Board's ex-
pense, but in enhancing the spiritual life of the parish. A
letter of thanks from the Bishop of Newcastle, under
whom George had worked from his Monkseaton days,
was both warm and personal.

Thank you for telling me privately about your accep-
tance of the work in Newfoundland. I hope with all my
heart that things will go splendidly happily with you in
it all.... May I say straight out how grateful I am, under
God, for your ministry over these years in the diocese. I
am, of course, thinking of Falstone, but, not least, am I
thinking of all you have achieved in the building up of
the Church in Choppington. You will not, I know, wish
me to be over effusive, but I wanted to say how deeply
grateful I have always been, and still am.

On referring to his own imminent departure from
Newcastle as bishop of another diocese, Bishop Hudson
speaks of the personal happiness "to which you and yours
have so lovingly contributed."

Despite the domestic upheaval of the first two years in
Choppington George and Elna found their leaving painful. Not only were they leaving the parish that had become
their home, but Elna was leaving her native Northumberland for a different life on the edge of the new world. And
how would the children, who were after all English children, take the move from their friends and schools to a
distant land? Christine, ten, and Alison, seven, to the relief
of their parents shrieked with delight. They were going to
a land of adventure etched on their minds by their father's
bedtime stories. To a land of long summer days searching
for crabs and tansies on beaches far more exciting than
Northumberland's; catching conners and tomcods over
the wharf, and watching millions of capelin swim by; to
Christmas concerts and janneying for ten long nights and
then to sledding in snow as deep as your head; back to
monster whales puffing in the tickle, to thousands of
curious seals poking their noses out of the water and to
forests of wild animals. "When on driving home in the car
one day we were told that we were going to live in New-

foundland," Christine remembers, "it was like news that we were going to paradise." It was not easy to match her father's stories with the sidewalks of Forest Road, St. John's.

By June 1957 the vicar had said goodbye to his flock in his last service on June 23 and the children to their friends, while Elna had separated essential worldly goods from what had to be left behind. They were driven to Liverpool by brother Harry in the fine Singer car he had bought from them. While awaiting embarkation at Liverpool on June 25 George wrote a farewell to the Choppington parish magazine. Containing interesting facts and expressive of his sense of mission to the church, the letter merits citing at some length.

> Never before have we as a family done anything so hard and emotionally difficult [as leaving Choppington]. The kindness shown to us...has indicated beyond comprehension the best side of the English character and left an impression on our hearts and minds which is truly indelible. The climax of all this was on Sunday, 23rd June, with that memorable last Eucharist and the solemn Evensong with its intercession and thanksgivings uniting us all in spirit on the eve of our separation in body.

After thanking parishioners for the gift of £53 and the churchwardens for their kind words the letter continues.

> Over the past five years I have tried to do my best.... In various ways I have been in contact with the larger public. I baptised 517 infants, married 168 couples and laid 220 people to rest. In so far as I was informed, I have tried to look after the sick with their communion and to comfort the bereaved. Loving youth and desiring that they be given every opportunity to appreciate the

things of the spirit I have striven by patience and industry to guide them through their teens.... The bits and
pieces fit together to give us all as a family a sure
conviction that our years at Choppington have been the
happiest of all.... For now, farewell and every blessing
from Mrs. Earle, Christine, Alison and Peter and from
yours sincerely,

                    G. Halden Earle.

Queen's College Provost

The College to which George returned in 1957 after an eighteen-year absence was essentially the one he had left in 1939. The old wooden buildings on Forest Road were both inadequate for college facilities and also in bad repair, while the Principal's Lodge to which George took his family had been unofficially condemned as a fire trap. For that, and other reasons, serious thought had been given to closing the College as early as the decade following World War I. In January 1967 on the eve of the College's moving to new buildings on the Memorial University campus, George saluted its spirit and its state of decay. Three of the six verses read:

> While Canada her birthday keeps
> Old Queen's prepares for death;
> When Canada her harvest reaps
> Old Queen's will gasp for breath.
> We love thee but pray thee
> To draw thy dying breath.

> Though rain pours through thy chapel walls
> And coals refuse to burn,
> Though students shiver in thy halls
> And find it hard to learn.
> We love thee, we now see
> The end for which we yearn.

Somewhere my love is rising fast
As my old love departs;
The new is being built to last
The old is breaking hearts.
We love thee, we pity
Thy old and creaking parts.

Provost, Queen's College, 1965.

By the time George arrived as Principal there was also growing concern about the small number of candidates being attracted to the ministry and about the adequacy of training in a small college with only two or three teachers and in isolation from the enriching influence of a university. Indeed, to the new principal back from studies and parishes in England, some of the students seemed to be not only parochial but anti-academic. After one such student expressed aversion to having to take such subjects as philosophy and sociology when he had thought he was a theology student, the Principal reached for his poet's pen. Two of the verses of "I'm in Theology" (Tune: "The Old Gray Mare") read:

> I don't want to ponder philosophy,
> Ponder philosophy, ponder philosophy,
> I don't want to ponder philosophy,
>   I'm in Theology.
>
> I don't want to swot sociology,
> Swot sociology, swot sociology,
> I don't want to swot sociology,
>   I'm in Theology.

Thus the inadequacy of the old facilities and the growing feeling after Memorial University College became a university in 1949 that students would benefit from a more academic milieu led to consideration of building new facilities on the Memorial campus. The idea was approved in 1961 and ratified in 1963. It was an idea to which the new principal turned with enthusiasm. In a 1966 report, prepared partly for use in fund raising, Earle summarized the reasons for moving the College to the University campus:

> It is isolated from the University owing to its location and is the only theological college in Canada far removed from the campus. As an affiliated institution with courses required at the University and in the near future many more courses in the proposed Department of Theological Studies [Religious Studies], this distance of over 2½ miles is a stumbling-block.... The proximity of the new Queen's to the Roman Catholic and United Church residences should, in this oecumenical age,

make for a united Christian witness on campus without in any sense segregating the students from the University family.

Supervising the move to the Memorial campus and fund raising throughout the Province would be Earle's distinctive contributions to Queen's during a principalship of twenty-two years. It was partly for this achievement that he was made a canon of the Cathedral of St. John the Baptist in 1971. The new facility was opened for the term 1967-68. The official opening, presided over by Bishop R.L. Seaborn, took place on November 1, 1968, and was addressed by Dr. Leslie Harris, then Dean of Arts and Science at Memorial and later President. The Provost's (Earle's title from 1965) contribution to the ceremony was a reading from Proverbs and Plato's *Republic*, and the composition of a hymn for the occasion.

> Lord Jesus, bless Queen's College
> On campus and on trial,
> To change with changing knowledge
> And not the Good defile.
> Where Feild and Spencer laboured
> To train our pioneers,
> Thy Church in days more favoured
> Remembers leaner years.
>
> From far across the ocean
> The early students came
> With vision and devotion,
> To learn and spread Thy Name;
> Led on by clear vocation
> They worked with mind and hand,
> That faith and education
> Be sown in Newfoundland.
>
> In journeys long and weary
> By foot and boat and sleigh,

In places bleak and dreary
They visited to pray;
In teaching, guiding, healing
They saw life's purpose clear,—
In faith and fellow-feeling
Their people's lot to share.

And thus, Thy Church as leader
Brought learning, truth and light
Through parson and lay reader
To island, cove and bight;
The men-folk gave free labour,
The women cooked and sewed,
And each one helped his neighbour
To share life's heavy load.

May we, their heirs, be standing
For what is true and just,
Gain wisdom, understanding,
And guard the past in trust.
So, bless Queen's College, Saviour,
And us in mind and hand,
By learning and behaviour
To strengthen Newfoundland.

The cost of the new facility was estimated at $2 million, half of which Newfoundland parishes would be asked to contribute. To this end the Provost took extensive leaves to visit virtually every parish in the Province, thereby incidentally adding to his great store of knowledge of Newfoundland.   Speaking at a Queen's College Alumni banquet in 1987 he noted that his awareness of Queen's began in 1919 at the age of five. "My first awareness was financial — I was made to pledge 5¢ a year" to the College. This was in reference to his joining the "Guild of St. Andrew, for Queen's College," one condition of admission, written on the membership card, being a pledge "To subscribe at least 5 cents a year until I am 10 years old and 10 cents a year from 10 to 14 years of age to the Guild." No doubt it was this pledge that inspired his fund-raising slogan in parishes, "A nickel a day for three years."

George found fund raising the most taxing of his duties. Although the new College complex would include two residences, Feild Hall and Spencer Hall, for outport students attending the College and Memorial University, he was especially apprehensive about soliciting funds in outport parishes. As he told an audience in St. John's in 1966, "It will not be easy to convince all outport people that a set of new buildings in St. John's is a necessity or deserving of their charity." His set speech, sprinkled with humour for the occasion, about the need for new facilities on the Memorial campus was therefore first presented to St. John's audiences. At Feild Hall in 1965, where Bishop Feild and Bishop Spencer colleges staged plays to raise money for the new Queen's, he turned his hand to verse.

> When Queen's got old and out of date
> The thought went forth — to relocate
> And place it nearer MUN,
> To give a better chance to men
> To learn, discuss and mix and think
> And form a strong abiding link
> With students of all kinds and bents
> And variegated temperaments.

The next two verses tell how after "we sought and got the Synod vote," talking "started all anew." Frustration with debates and delays finds expression in the fourth verse.

> But thoughts that we should soon begin
> Were tantamount to mortal sin;
> For Anglicans, it's wrong to act
> Until each figure and each fact

Are weighed and weighed for years and years,
Until no one has doubts and fears,
Till those who wished to go ahead
In interest are cold and dead.

The last verse thanks the staffs of Feild and Spencer.

And now the Feild and Spencer caste
Have joined the tour with joyful blast.
To light the stage and paint them all
We have Miss Norman and Miss Hall;
The strong support we now uncover
Of Misses Thomas, Jones and Glover.
To heads of schools and staff and crew,
To one and all — our thanks to you.

One of George's first pitches for funds was made in 1960. While it came naturally to him to inject humour into his speeches he must have found it peculiarly helpful on this occasion. After outlining the needs for a new building, he noted that "I seem to be taking a long time to get to the point, like the young man who was trying to propose to a young woman. After several feeble efforts he said, 'I don't seem to be making much progress.' 'No,' she replied, 'but you are holding your own.'" The cost of the new facility, he explained, will be $2 million. "How can I go around New-foundland and tell this? It needs courage and faith. Many will refuse. But it must be done."

Over a two-year period George visited almost all par-ishes on the Island and in Labrador. In the early summer of 1965 he travelled by motorboat along the south coast from Bay L'Argent to Ramea and Burgeo. Along with two crew members, his brother Charlie accompanied him on this trip and found that "George was not comfortable at fund raising." It must have been a welcome respite to be able to spend a few days fishing at Conne River.

On July 19, immediately after his return from the trip,

George chose to make his observations of south coast communities the subject of a talk on the CBC's "Morning Devotions." He began with examples of abandoned or dying communities. "In many cases the property built up by generations of hardworking fishermen is left to decay. Lovely churches, schools, lodges, dwelling houses, shops and stages are rotting." In Stone's Cove, which had been abandoned the year before, George "had the sad task, with the Rector of Belleoram, of deconsecrating the fine church" built in 1927 in replacement of an earlier church built in 1898. In Anderson's Cove a church towed twenty miles over water from an abandoned community "still lies lop-sidedly just up from the landwash because suddenly that community has decided to fold up" (which it did the next year). Several other communities, Earle noted, had no future.

A third of the way through his talk George put the question that must have occurred to some listeners, "What has all this to do with Morning Devotions?" The answer, he said, is that "people caught up in what is called the march of progress...have to leave solid communities because they are small and go to larger ones where the community spirit is often weak. We are creatures of earth and get tied to a humble dwelling and small plot, and familiar fishing grounds and a village church." The people, he continued, have become "wedded to simple things like good drinking water or a fine view or the particular sound of the surf or even the colour of the rocks, not to mention their home and garden." The talk ended with prayer for the older people "dragging their anchor" and set adrift, and for the younger people that "they continue to hold fast to the faith of their fathers." That simple morning devotion is one of George's most telling statements of his conviction that people must always be seen as "creatures of earth" and that, therefore, the ministry should emphasize the practical Christianity of Canon Richards in northern New-foundland and Father Jackson in Monkseaton.

It was of course this emphasis, the choice of St. James over St. Paul, the belief that it is by good works that faith is made perfect, that George Halden Earle brought to the education and training of young men at Queen's College. While insisting that students "ponder philosophy, swot sociology and study psychology," he nonetheless was un-wavering in the belief that only love for people and a deep desire to help them in their daily rounds could make effective vicars of Christ. In a talk to Queen's Alumni in 1987, Earle posed the question, "Can anyone really be *trained* for the ministry?" Of his own student days he remarked, "I'm not so stunned as to think that Queen's was training us well for the ministry." Recalling his work with Father Jackson, the "good works" rector in Monksea-ton, he said that the best training comes with involvement in both the life of a parish and community. "A person," he concluded, "with love of people in his heart . . . and a sense of service in his soul, and some learning in his head, can accomplish much in a parish situation where people live, marry and die."

George's forte was not fund raising or even general administration, but teaching and rapport with students. Whether he was writing about Change Islands people or dealing with students, he was always fascinated with what psychologists came to call individual differences, learning from students as he had from characters in Change Islands and Fogo. In speaking on Queen's College to the Kiwanis Club of St. John's in 1967 under the title "Fun with Stu-dents and Others," he noted that, "In the dining hall I rotate students so that during the year I sit at the table with them all. We exchange yarns. I get anecdotes and pull legs. It is a great opportunity." Of course close association with the Provost put students at risk of having their foibles and

Fogo, 1957. L to R: George's father, Christine, Peter, George, Alison, George's mother.

misdemeanours exposed and even appear in bits of doggerel. Like the chaps, the Kiwanis Club was told, who used
to sneak out in the evening break to phone their girlfriends; the boaster of great hunting skills who got lost in
the woods; the outport fellow who fell into the hands of
the police after going to the country with a moose licence
and coming back with a duck, his blunder later exposed in
verse, titled "Alec Get Your Gun."

> I'll tell you the story of Alec
> Who found himself home on the loose;
> He thought he would go to the country
> To look for and shoot at a moose.

His licence was back at the College,
But Alec went out just the same
With luncheon and rifle and bullets
To clobber his innocent game.

The day wearied on unmolested
For Alec was having no luck;
Then suddenly out of the bushes
There flew up a fine-looking duck.

Then Alec saw looming two charges —
With little reward in his sack —
For seeking a moose without licence
And shooting a duck in the back.

He shared up the duck with his parents,
Recovered his licence from Mun;
He's ready to do some more hunting
When the Mounties return him his gun.

Then there were the poor lad who saw no need to "swot philosophy" and the unfortunate fellow who late one night "sneaked back into the College through the skylight right into my arms, and who thereafter caused no trouble." Of the two students, one High Church the other Low, who began to court two sisters, George quipped, "They're strangers in Churchmanship, brothers in love." The pious will take comfort in the fact that not all of these culprits were divinity students. Nonetheless it was the underlying point of George's talk to the Kiwanis Club that fun and humour ought to have a central place in the church. "Many people," he noted, "still equate laughter with insincerity, and the poker face with sincerity."

After an annual dance at which the Provost was invited to be master of ceremonies he recorded his observations in "The Library Floor."

Oh! This is the place where the Queen's students
    gather
Just once in the year for to dance and to roar;
With books covered over they all are in clover
As they congregate here on the Library floor.

Some are showing affection while others are laughin'
For some have their sweethearts and others have not;
They smoke and eat candy and look nice and dandy
While waiting to waltz or to jive or to trot.

The author of "The Squid-Jiggin' Ground" might not
have regarded this as great poetry but he would have been
flattered by the emulation.

Canon Earle held the liberal theological and doctrinal
view that one would normally expect from a person who
is more disposed to good works than to fencing in the
arena of metaphysical speculation. In what sounded like a
quip but was in fact a deeply held position, when I asked
him about doctrinal differences between High and Low
Church his quick reply was, "You Dissenters bring up too
many ifs and buts. Only young people split hairs in theology." We passed on to another topic.

Nowhere does Earle's liberalism find more explicit
expression than in a talk on religious toleration he gave to
an assembly of Salvation Army people when he was a
member of the Commission for Church Union examining
the possibility of union between the Anglican and United
churches. A scholarly, historical talk, "Religious Toleration
and the Newfoundland Perspective," after tracing the history of religious intolerance to the fourth century when the
church accepted the patronage of Constantine I and in
doing so became an arm of the state, it concludes, "Christianity, which claims to be the only true religion, has always
been dogmatically intolerant." Religious intolerance fol-
lows, the author noted, "when you are sure beyond doubt

that you have the truth and the others are completely wrong." The question whether religion can flourish without dogma is happily one that need not be raised here.

The same distaste for dogma was expressed more light-heartedly in a 1987 talk to Queen's alumni when he was reviewing his years as a student. Recalling how the College paper, *Live Wire*, which he edited for two years, had once been 'scrapped' for stirring up controversial issues he noted, "This was when the division between High and Low, Catholic and Protestant, was very important. It caused more trouble than the meals or lack of freedom or rigid discipline." By my time, George added, these issues had been put on the back burner "and I got the boils, which hurt as much whether you were High or Low." Reference to boils was not just a touch of George's earthy humour, but a serious reaffirmation of the "Morning Devotions" view that religion must not begin and end with disembodied spirits and recondite speculation, but with people as "creatures of earth."

It was mainly because of Earle's liberal views that he was such an enthusiastic member of the Commission on union with the United Church of Canada. His experience in England had reinforced his conviction that union, not only with the United Church but with several others, was both desirable and possible. As he said of his experience in Falstone, "Before the age of ecumenism we 'ecumenized;' before the day of house services and non-church building congregations we [the Presbyterian minister and himself] did it in farmers' sitting rooms and even in the Kielder castle lounge." In both Falstone and Choppington Methodists regularly came to the parish church for baptism and marriages. True enough, Earle quipped in his address on religious toleration, they were not the kind of Methodists who "came to Newfoundland in the middle of the nineteenth century and who didn't like us much." As it turned

out, his optimism was not well-placed. The marriage of
one of his theological students to a United Church woman
was the occasion of his "The Principles of Union," a parody
of the churches' tortured discussions.

> Some twenty men took twenty years
> Of study, prayer and thought
> To formulate the principles
> On which the Churches ought
> To come together by and by
> In one agreed belief,
> And put the Bishops in their place
> And give the Church relief.
>
> They say 'twill take us twenty years
> To work the document;
> To get a Book of Common Prayer
> And common hymns for Lent;
> To unify the Ministries,
> See where the layman stands,
> And put the women in their place
> And who will lay on hands.
>
> And so we see some forty years
> On principles and plan,
> Commissions working to effect
> The will of God and man.
> And yet a membership of two
> Can do the work of ten
> In twenty days of love and faith,—
> When Betty gets with Ben.

Along with his primary work as Provost of Queen's,
Canon Earle served as chaplain to Anglican students at the
University, and as the College's representative on the
University Senate; on the Anglican school board and the
Executive Committee of Synod and on such community

organizations as the Canadian Mental Health Association and the Kiwanis Club; and preached in numerous churches throughout Newfoundland and the Maritimes.

It was during his early years at Queen's College that George's celebrated after-dinner speaking career was launched. His first humorous address was given at a graduation banquet for Memorial University students in 1961. Having long been amazed by the solemn, boring lectures he had heard at school exercises and graduations, he had resolved that, should the opportunity arise, he would try a light-hearted approach. "I didn't want to give you a lecture," he told the graduates and dignitaries, "but merely to share the glow and glory of this lighter side of Graduation Day." He hoped that he was "not misjudging the atmosphere on speaking in poor taste on this great occasion."

The style of this first after-dinner speech, with its skilful blending of humorous anecdote and pointed moral, was similar to the thousand that were to follow. It began, "I feel a great bit honoured and a little bit scared." His purported temerity in addressing such a sophisticated audience reminded him of an Irishman's fright in World War II when "a bullet went in me chest and came out the back." In that case, remarked his observant friend, "the bullet would have gone through your heart and killed you." "Yes, but me heart was in me mouth at the time." Following this joke there was an observation on the importance not only of what one says but how it is said. The father was right in coaching his son, "don't say to a homely girl 'Your face would stop the clock,' but 'When I look into your eyes time stands still.' "

In public speaking, George continued, intonation is crucial. A senior physician, giving his new assistant lessons in public relations, advised that, since doctors couldn't remember the sex of all the babies they delivered, it was enough to greet mother and baby, "That *is* a baby." Not long afterwards the assistant greeted a young mother with her baby in the perambulator, "Is *that* a baby?" After a few more illustrations of the problems semantics can cause, the short talk concluded with the admonition to launch out into the deep and, reflecting the practical Christianity that marked George's priesthood, "to serve God by serving humanity."

It was also in his early years as Provost of Queen's College that Canon Earle wrote his twelve-verse patriotic song "Come Home to Old Newfy." The poem has an interesting genesis and history. The Smallwood government had declared 1966 Come Home Year in the hope of enticing thousands of expatriates home as the kickoff for an ambitious tourist program. The announcement "got me thinking about Old Newfoundland," as George was later to tell the Newfoundland Historical Society, "and what people who had left years ago would want to come back to." Recalling that in the North of England, "the past, even the distant past, was ever present," he wondered whether he could "make it live here." And so he resolved to contribute to the nostalgia of the year by calling up his poetic muse.

The first opportunity to present the poem came at a flipper banquet at the Crow's Nest, a St. John's club for military officers, in April 1965. Later he scribbled on his notes for the evening, "I received a standing ovation and this gave me the green light to go ahead." The green light led him to Smallwood's office and the suggestion that the government might wish to use "Come Home" in its advertising. After the Premier and cabinet expressed delight in it, George and his sister Mabel (Kirby) set the poem to music, an adaptation of an old song Grandfather Earle used to sing. Thousands of copies of "Come Home" as a song sheet were then distributed by the Tourist Bureau to schools and a variety of other groups, while hundreds of copies were sold. Except for his books, "Come Home" is the only work that George had copyrighted. It appears in his *Old Foolishness or Folklore?* (Harry Cuff Pubs. 1987).

Nostalgic and romantic, "Come Home to Old Newfy" draws on most of the elements that would characterize Earle's copious output of old foolishness or folklore over the next thirty years. Some verses stir memories of mug-ups and scoffs and of subliminal tastes and smells:

> Come home to old Newfy, the land of your birth,
> From your lands of adoption all over the earth;
> Come home to the smell of the kelp and the fir,
> To the taste of the caplin, the lobster and turr.
> Come home to the scruncheons, the praties and fish
> All mixed with the brewis in the fisherman's dish.
>
> Come home to the cod tongues, the breeches and
>   sounds
> And eat them in motorboats out on the grounds,
> We'll keep in cold storage some flippers and birds
> And Newfoundland rabbit and moose from the
>   herds.
> Come home to the fish cake, the rounder and scrod
> And pea soup with doughboys and chowder with
>   cod.

The song promises a return to childhood pleasures.

> Come home to the hummock, the wood and the wild
> And traipse through the pathways you made as a
>   child.
> The boat's on the collar, the trout in the stream,
> The whort and the bakeapple waiting for cream.
> Come home to the landwash, the ponds and the bars
> And bide till it's duckish and wait for the stars.

Townies returning to St. John's are offered old scenes and major new ones.

> Come to St. John's with her Narrows and Forts,
> To this oldest of all North American ports;
> Her front is some altered — and so is her back —
> She flies the new flag by the old Union Jack.
> Come home to her streets and her lanes and her hills,
> The Lake and Regatta give wonderful thrills.

On George's retirement from Queen's in 1979 he and Elna moved to a home they had bought a few years earlier in Topsail. Meanwhile the three children who had left England for paradise in 1957 had grown up and settled in St. John's.

Earle siblings. L to R: (Back), Jean, Charles, Fred, George, Ethel. (Front), June, Gertrude, Edna, Mabel. (Harry is missing from the photo.)

Storyteller

Although Canon Earle was a distinguished churchman, and head of Queen's College for twenty-two years, it was as a humorist that he was best known in Newfoundland and beyond. In demand as an after-dinner speaker for more than three decades following his return from England in 1957, he estimated a few years ago that he had given over a thousand speeches to audiences from Ferryland to Port Aux Basques and from Halifax to St. Andrews, New Brunswick. Perhaps even more interesting was the variety of groups he chose to address, ranging from Rhodes Scholars to a funeral planning association, the Salmon Association of Newfoundland to the Atlantic Fruit and Vegetable Association, the Knights of Columbus to the Allied Beauty Association, and from a convention of bakers to the Atlantic Provinces Jewellers.

Canon Earle rarely turned down an opportunity to speak before ill health slowed him down in later years. Yet, the talks often involved tiring travel, the ambience of meetings was not always one to uplift the spirits, and generally the only material reward was another pen and pencil set or a photograph of the community he was speaking in. Why, then, did he accept the thousand invitations? One answer is suggested by the fact that whether the talks were given to the Canadian Press in St. John's or beauticians in Halifax his topic in perhaps ninety percent of the speeches was Newfoundland folklore or 'old foolishness.' As a proud patriot he felt the deep need both to celebrate and to record our heritage. Moreover, like all speakers who can move audiences, he relished the applause and was stimulated by it. In the end perhaps he became an after-dinner speaker simply because he couldn't silence the imp that his teachers had discovered in him. He himself often spoke of humour as a divine gift, and would have appreciated the excuse four-year-old Geoffrey Downey gave his father, Dr. James Downey, when accused of talking too much, "It's God's fault. He keeps tickling me and makes me talk."

While George sometimes raised the question of the nature of humour, and gave talks under the titles "Laughter" and "A Twinkle in the Eye," he never felt it useful to offer a serious analysis of it. Explanations of humour have varied from the physiological — the view that facial muscle contractions are the cause of laughter, not a concomitant of it; to the metaphysical, according to which humour is an antidote to man's sense of mortality; to the psychological or pre-emptive, that is, making oneself or one's people the butt of ridicule before others do so; and to the most recent theory that humour is engendered by excess of vitamin D. The good thing about the last theory is that humour can be dispensed by drugstores, the only drawback that medicare covers only necessities. None of these theories are taken seriously by humorists themselves. One of many problems with theory was nicely put by the editors of a book of Australian jokes, "As soon as you start thinking about the construction and purpose of a joke the humour evaporates. It's like confusing sexual intercourse with gynecology or art with criticism."

One of the fascinating questions about humour is why some people are possessed of it, others not. Insofar as George tried to explain his own humour he attributed it to close observation of a people. In his essay "Humour" he wrote, "You see the Newfoundlander — in my case the rural Newfoundlander — as a character. You understand his speech, you notice his reactions, you spot his reasoning and feel it, you observe his defence mechanisms or natural wit or gift of exaggeration or use of imagination and so forth." But why are some observers funny and many others not? Perhaps the explanation lies in George's own observation that "if beauty lies in the eye of the beholder it is equally true that humour lies in the ear of the hearer." The characters in Change Islands are funny only if they are *seen* as funny. This is what Anthony Burgess meant in remarking that, "There is nothing intrinsically funny in anything" (*Little Wilson and Big God*). The humorous eye doesn't just see; like a camera filter it selects. Still, in the end perhaps Earle's explanation of his own humorous bent is as good as any. "I guess that I was born a bit of an imp."

But humour, like garden flowers, flourishes only with nutrients and good soil. George Earle's impishness was stimulated by his father, whose forte was mimicry and ballad singing, and especially by his grandfather Earle. Of his grandfather he wrote (in "Relations"): "Grandfather was a character. I used to be told that I got my 'badness' from him. He was always telling stories, was musical, a well-known entertainer, and, as people used to say, a concert unto himself. He sang the songs of Harry Lauder and many others I have forgotten. He had a gramophone and lots of records and learnt many songs from them." The essay ends with a song his grandfather often sang, which is known under several titles including, "The Longest Name Song," and which "is dedicated to my grandfather's memory and his great sense of humour."

My father and mother were excellent folks;
They spent all their time in practical jokes;

And when I was born they were both of one mind;
They said I could have all the names they could find;
And so they considered, as wise as could be,
And this is the handle they stuck onto me.

Among the twenty-eight names given the child and
which make up the chorus are, Jonathan, Joseph, Jere-
miah, Hyman, Tyman, Nicholas, Pat, Christopher, Dick,
Jehosaphat. When George and his sister Mabel wrote the
tune for "Come Home to Old Newfy" George dedicated it
to his grandfather.

Given the fact that when grandfather Earle was singing such songs and telling his young grandson stories he
had lost part of his jaw in cancer surgery and was regarded
by the young boy as "a kind of cripple," his humour must
have made a profound impression on George. Profound
enough that among his papers is a copy of a song "sung
often by Grandpa Earle at concerts." Titled "Where Did
You Get That Hat?," it seems to have been robbed of its
humour by time. The first of five verses reads:

Now how I came to get that 'tis very strange and
    funny:
Grandfather died and left me his property and
    money;
And when the will it was read out, they told me
    straight and flat,
If I would have his money, I must always wear his hat.

Bound by the terms of the will, the poor chap was
thereafter the object of ridicule. In the words of the chorus,
"Where'er I go they shout, 'Hello, where did you get that
hat?'" George's family lived near the grandparents and, he
recalled, "we were in and out many times daily." That
young George, not yet fourteen, was allowed to smoke
while listening to his grandfather's jokes and yarns added

to his pleasure and pleasant memories. (The grandparents' large home, built in 1888, is now a popular B & B with the name Seven Oakes.)

Ted Russell was another influence. True enough, the twinkle that bespoke George's humour was already pronounced before he became a student of Russell's in Fogo in 1928. But in later years he mentioned the eagerness with which he had listened to Russell swapping yarns with his father and his fascination with his teacher's old foolishness. Later, when George and Russell were students at Memorial College, the two met often and "exchanged yarns." By the time George returned from England, Russell, his senior by a decade, had proven through his CBC chronicles that tiny Pigeon Inlets were rich in drama and humour. Given that Canon Earle sometimes expressed uneasiness about making old foolishness an avocation, it is possible that had not Russell legitimized folklore and local humour he himself would have shrunk from the role.

The community of Change Islands itself seems to have been congenial to humour. Not only George Earle but other natives remember it as having a marked sense of fun. In his "Outport Memories" (*Book of Newfoundland,* bk IV), Art Scammell contends that Change Islands was "especially blessed" with a penchant for the practical joke and humour. In the same volume of the *Book of Newfoundland* Earle also recalls how "There was plenty of room for gaiety...from Monday to Saturday you never knew what prankster would be at work to add colour to life and give spice to the atmosphere." Change Islands, he told the *Evening Telegram* in 1979, "was the proper atmosphere for a boy with a sense of humour to be bred and nurtured in." The community, he told me in 1999, "was swarming with characters." Both Scammell and Earle insist that the characters immortalized in "The Squid-Jiggin' Ground" and elsewhere were real people, all of them from Skipper John Chaffey to old Jacob Steele, from Uncle Bob Hawkins to the red-headed Tory.

Change Islands, George's fictional Mussel Gut, "one of the funniest communities on the northeast coast," was his Pigeon Inlet. The winter twine lofts were theatres of wit and storytelling and rehearsal rooms for the community's Earles and Scammells. Other venues are remembered in George's "Come Home to Old Newfy."

> Come home to the shop and the squid jiggin' ground,
> The lodge and the corner where men hang around;
> The fishermen gather outside the Church gate
> For a smoke or a quid and a chat as they wait.
> Come home to the wharf when the coastal boat blows
> And meet all the liveyers assembled in rows.

Even after allowing for the colouring that time and distance often give to experience, it does seem that Earle and Scammell were justified in acclaiming Change Islands as a particularly fun-loving and humorous people. In his *Fun on the Rock* (1983) Herbert L. Pottle, in offering a sociology of Newfoundland humour, singles out for scrutiny Upper Island Cove and Change Islands as communities "particularly notable for their humour." While he expresses doubt that he can explain why these two communities were so notably given to fun and humour, he is confident that he can "open up some leads." The leads are that both communities, as isolated places, developed a sense of humour in reaction to "the shock of being wrenched from their trans-Atlantic roots;" as their "defence against the encircling hostile elements;" and that, cohesive in cultural background (the West Country of England) and religion, they were natural nurseries of storytelling. There are several flaws in this analysis, but it is enough to mention one. Even if we allow the three conditions to stand as facts, clearly they are not peculiar to Upper Island Cove and Change Islands; they are found in many Newfoundland communities, which on Pottle's analysis should have been equally fun-loving and humorous. As George remarked in a letter to me in April 1985, "a lot of Pottle's good material was fooled up and a lot of it should have been omitted."

I had conversations with Pottle about his theory, having long been interested in his question. Why was it that Change Islands seemed to produce a disproportionate number of people caught up in old foolishness? My own theory came to me in a flash just before sunset July 28, 1976 as my brothers Ed and Winston and crewmen Don Cameron and Cousin Don Poole were discussing the question on the *Shamrock II* anchored at Change Islands after a day at the Funks. Realizing for the first time that George Earle, Ted Russell, Art Scammell and Otto Tucker all had a connection with Change Islands, Earle and Scammell as natives, Tucker as a former teacher there, and Russell as husband of a native, it dawned on me that it was the noxious vapor from a nearby marsh that had addled their brains and driven them to old foolishness. That theory is perhaps as good as any. Still, sociologists and sailors should leave humour to the poets, content to know that, like the wind, it bloweth where it listeth, none knowing whence it cometh or whither it goeth.

While Earle showed little interest in general theories of humour, he always insisted that his own humour derived from close observation of character. "Over the past quarter of a century," he wrote in his essay on humour, "I have given well over a thousand after-dinner speeches, and if I have succeeded at all it's because I am more interested in culture and character than in jokes." The point was amplified in a 1976 speech he gave to the Humanities Association of Canada. "I have noted many of the characteristics of the Newfoundlander. These I try to convey in after-dinner speeches, with humorous anecdotes. Sometimes ... the dialect, sometimes the reasoning, sometimes the repartee and sometimes a misunderstanding of words or an ambiguous use of language." Since character is moulded by history and geography, he reminded students at Memorial University, it is reasonable to believe that there is a distinctive Newfoundland character, and observations made on extensive travel abroad confirm the belief.

If it is true, as Earle believed, that character is a product not only of genes and history but also of geography, it would follow that in theory Mussel Gut is different from Scilly Cove and considerably different from Ferryland. Earle's answer to that theoretical question is that centuries of life on an isolated island have made Newfoundlanders of us all. And several writers, including George Allan England, Julian Moreton, Farley Mowat and J.R. Smallwood, have recognized that fact, some going so far as to refer to Newfoundlanders as a race. George's wide and intimate knowledge of Newfoundland certainly made him an expert witness. As he noted in 1975, "I have covered most parts of the Island and some parts of Labrador and have been in contact with hundreds of young people who come from all over..., bringing their dialect and local expressions with them" (*Book of Newfoundland*, bk VI).

Canon Earle's humour is harder to expose than, say, Ray Guy's or Ed Smith's. In the first place, since the after-dinner speech was its main vehicle, much of it has been lost to the record. Secondly, whereas crafted humour seems to be the primary aim of the funny writing of Ray Guy and Ed Smith, the humour in Earle's speeches is incidental to another purpose. He certainly enjoyed making people laugh, but the overriding purpose of the great majority of his speeches was, like Russell's chronicles, to celebrate Newfoundland history and culture, and to record a way of life whose passing he lamented. There are therefore large sections of his humorous speeches — and essays — that are not, when taken in isolation from the whole, funny or intended to be funny. As he himself remarked about speech-making, "There is no need to laugh in every line."

Earle himself was strong in the view that humour is not simply a string of funny stories or jokes a la the Newfy joke books that tourists gobble up in tens of thousands. Thus of Amos and Andy of radio fame he remarked in "Humour" that their brand of humour "was based less on comedy and jokes than on the creation of character. Had they merely strung off one joke after another (corny or not) they would not have lasted so long." To be fully appreciated, then, Canon Earle's funny stories must be read or heard as illustrating a point and as true to his characters. For him humour was the preferred expression of understanding and love.

The vehicle of Earle's best humour was the language of Change Islands (Mussel Gut), which includes both West Country dialect, now a dead language in England, imported words and expressions given new meanings here, and even words invented in Newfoundland. It is in the West Country dialect that characters in "Henry Jarge's Giant Squid" ask Uncle Jarge about the giant squid he found.

> "Tell us about that gurt big vish you zeed up een the Run,
> For some o' we believe 'tis lies that people stritch fer fun."
> "No lies at all," said Uncle Jarge, and that was all he said,
> Except to add "the ruddy vish had bin a good spurt dead."

When further pressed he scratched his head and
  rolled around his quid,
"Altho' his tail was rotted off I knows he was a squid;
Tho' he wuz dead a spurt and 'off' — I'm not now
  tellin' yarns —
I'll tell ee how I knowed en, boys, I knowed en be his
  harns."

Dialect is also an ingredient in the humour of "Kip
Stiddy Parson," Earle's story of a solicitous Anglican who
swatted a mosquito on his parson's forehead.

"Kip stiddy Parson Martin, zir,
Thur's a nipper on yer vard,
Don't think I wants to knock 'ee out
Or even hit 'ee hard;
I only wants that skitty squat
So he will never bite
And put en whur all skits should be —
Completely out of sight."

When the layman's hand "come down a vicious
swipe/that staggered Parson Jarge" the devout Anglican
was embarrassed but not apologetic.

But when a nipper's on a vard
And ready fer to bite,
Respect for cloth and holiness
Comes second in the fight;
It makes no odds who owns the vard
Whur nippers choose to land
So, just bide stiddy clergyman,
Accept the layman's hand.

Local dialect also spiced much of Earle's prose. One of
his favourite observations was that, "whereas on the mainland, to be stunned you have to be kicked in the head, in
Newfoundland you can be born stunned." Another fa-

vourite, which always elicited hearty laughter, was the description of a person working more or less aimlessly as "just firkin around." The speeches are also sprinkled with local words such as crunnicks, prog and scrod. Audiences laughed at the image of an old codger "spellin' in crunnicks" to keep the fire going and at the idea of a teacher "being progged" by a local family. But, as I noted earlier, the multiplication of examples of Earle's humour out of context evokes the misleading image of a teller of jokes. Earle was not a Pat-and-Mike man.

There are, one wit remarked, three rules for creating humour, and none of them have been discovered. Why people find dialect funny is probably one of the mysteries. It may not be hard to understand why the Oxonian laughs at the Cockney, but it is surely puzzling why the Cockney laughs at himself. Liveyers in Mussel Gut no less than St. John's urbanites found Canon Earle's use of dialect funny. This phenomenon of a people's laughing at their own dialect was a matter of puzzlement to the celebrated Dor-

Conference of Atlantic premiers and New England governors. L to R: Premier Brian Peckford; Earle; Governor Brennan, Maine; Mrs. G.A. Winter.

set dialect poet, William Barnes (1801-86), whose use of local language evoked as much laughter in his native Blackmore Vale as it did in sophisticated Dorchester and Weymouth. Dialect is funny to its users only when it is an older language already giving place to a new, 'modern' and 'superior' one. Canon Earle, like the Reverend William Barnes, used old dialect when it was rapidly giving place to a new one, i.e. to standard English.

Canon Earle's humorous speeches sometimes drew on what he called the Newfoundlander's "gift of exaggeration." When it was rumoured that Uncle Jarge had caught a giant squid, "All kinds of stories spread around the islands of the bay/And everybody stretched a bit (as is the Newfy way)." In the end it was established that the squid was "as long as a piece of rope." George's favourite species of hyperbole was in the response he received to an inquiry in Mussel Gut about a very thin, skinny man he hadn't seen for many years. "Is he as thin as ever?" "Theen? He's so theen that he's got to open his mouth to get enough skin to shut his eyes."

Newfoundland's best known hyperbolist, Premier Smallwood, inspired one of Earle's cleverest pieces of doggerel. The March 6, 1966 *Evening Telegram* reported that during a debate on the budget the day before the Premier lambasted members of both sides of the House for their "chuckledheadedness and muddleheadedness" in voting against Confederation in 1948, adding that they "should carry their shame to their graves" and meanwhile "wrap themselves in sackcloth and ashes." This eloquent outburst moved Earle to write "Confederation Sinners."

> You chuckledheaded, muddleheaded, miserable
>   wretches,
> The shame of nineteen forty-eight will bring eternal
>   stretches

Of punishment and misery to everyone who gloated
That Newfoundland could stand alone — and can-
    vassed, lied and voted.

You hypocrites from sepulchres so glamorous and
    whited,
You suckers of a former age with prejudice so
    blighted,
You mortal sinners of this isle, both Liberals and
    Tories,
You, in your ignorance and sin, told endless lies and
    stories.

Look at your present jobs and cheques and feel your
    greasy pockets,
Your eyes should shut with guilt and shame and
    vanish in their sockets;
Should not the senior citizens, the unemployed and
    kiddies
You nearly robbed of benefits now give you all the
    diddies?

The only way to clean your graves and rectify your
    blindness
Is by a public penitence and public acts of kindness
On all the outport roads and lanes and pavement in
    the city,
And gaze at children all around with tenderness and
    pity.

And don't put on your Sunday best or uniforms with
    sashes
But wrap yourselves in dirty sacks and swob your-
    selves with ashes;
So, to your knees in sackcloth now, seek pardon from
    your nation
And grovel for the vote you cast against Confedera-
    tion.

Earle also took delight in toasting the natural wit of Newfoundlanders, illustrating his talks with examples heard or collected over the years. Asked why the church turned down the offer of a piece of land for a new cemetery, Uncle Henry replied, "Oh, 'twas too lonely for a cemetery." To a group of travellers criticizing the snail-pace of the Bonavista railway, a local character quipped, "I was on it once when a funeral passed us by." When one of two brothers owning a general store went to the Salvation Army and "got saved," and forthwith burnt the sinful stock of tobacco and playing cards, the second brother, asked when he was going to get saved, quipped, "I can't get saved—Jack didn't leave me anything to get saved on." One of George's favourite ripostes, told in his essay on "Humour," came from an outporter who was being accused of poor domestic economy. Although there was a tavern in his community he and his two or three friends regularly drove fifty miles for beer that was two cents a bottle cheaper. "You fellows," he was counselled, "is some stund thinking you're saving money. Sure don't you count the cost of gas?" "Yes, but you see we always drinks till we makes a profit." Such was Canon Earle's skill as a speaker that anecdotes seemed to pop out of the text as an essential part of it.

Brightening several of his talks were examples of unconscious humour. The bayman who took a case of rum and a loaf of bread on a moose hunting trip and was asked by his buddy, "What are you doing with all that bread?" The woman who on being asked whether her dog was a thoroughbred replied, "We're not sure; we knows his mother was a crackie, but we're not sure of his father"; and the woman who responded to the doctor's comment that he didn't like the look of her husband, "I don't either, but he was good to the children." A White Bay man, disgusted with the nasty taste of his latest batch of moonshine, confessed that "it was a relief when 'twas all gone."

George picked up some of his anecdotes from radio talk-shows and some from television. In his chapter on humour in *Old Foolishness or Folklore?* he told how on Bonfire Night one year he heard on television a CBC reporter asking a succession of children whether they knew who Guy Fawkes was and, getting no positive response, turned to an adult, "I bet you know who Guy Fawkes was?" "No, I wouldn't know; I'm from out of town." Admirers of the distinguished Canon would have taken delight in knowing that, after he retired, he was an avid listener to radio talk-shows, appreciated for their tortured and amusing language. One woman was so thrilled with her new hearing aid that when she first wore it, "it was an eye-opener." A regular caller, deploring the resettlement programs, ruefully reported that when he last visited his former home, "there was nothing left but an Anglican couple and a single cow." George's rich radio collection was kept in his files, most of it later appearing in his talks.

The Mussel Gut 'dialect,' like all local language, evolved not only to express literal meaning but to capture subtle nuances. As Earle's "The Whole Emmer" put it:

> In every land the people have
> Their own peculiar way
> Of showing thanks and gratitude
> By word or deed or pay;
> In every land each local place
> Invents a word or phrase
> That everyone can understand
> Without a paraphrase.
>
> The Newfoundlander years ago
> Expressed himself with hue,

He metaphored the local life
With phrases old and new;
So, everybody in the cove
Or in the bay or bight
Would understand the use of speech
And get the meaning right.

Perfect though it is for local communication, the language of Mussel Gut usually engenders cross-purpose conversation and humour when liveyers try to communicate with 'foreigners' from Ontario or Wisconsin. Earle's "The Yankee and the Newf" is a fine example. When the Yankee met up with an old codger hauling home a load of "crooked crunnicks on his slide," he "stuck his belly out a bit/And took his camera from his kit" and, after the manner of tourists everywhere, gushingly vented his curiosity about local ways.

He offered him a drink and smoke
Before the Newfy even spoke;
He talked a bit about the road
And then he spied the funny load.
"What's that you're dragging on that sleigh?"
"Var crunnicks, zir," the Newf did say.

"Var what?" the puzzled Yankee quizzed,
"Var starrigans some says they is."
"That's worse — how do you spell the stuff?"
"Well, on your back if you be tough,
But if you're weak in mind and heart
Don't spell 'em — haul 'em on a cart."

Although Earle looked askance at politics and especially at the succession of social and psychological theories parading as eternal verities, he rarely shone the torch of his humour on these proverbial sources of satire. The only examples of political humour — if indeed they can be

termed political — are his spoofing of Premier Smallwood's castigation of the "chuckledheaded, muddle-
headed, miserable wretches" who had voted against
Confederation and a roast of Smallwood at the Neptune
Theatre in Halifax. The roast was broadcast nationally by
the CBC in March 1977 when Smallwood was out of office
and succeeded as premier by Frank ('Frankie') Moores.
Other roasters were Jack Pickersgill, Richard Gwyn, Bryce
Mackasey, Gordon Pinsent and John Crosbie. Inexperi-
enced as a roaster, Earle "wasn't sure what to say" until "it
hit me that the one thing that the whole of Canada may be
acquainted with is the folksong 'I'se the B'y,' so I sat down
in my Hotel Nova Scotian room and made a parody of that
folksong." "Our B'y Joey" was the result.

> I'se the b'y that brought you in
> And took you from the lean years;
> I'se the b'y that burnt yer boats
> And took you to the cleaners.

> Chorus: Gifts to cover Come By Chance
> Grants galore for Erco,
> Power cheap for poor Quebec
> All around the circle.

> I don't want yer catchin' fish,
> You must make, or perish,
> Rubber boots and chocolate bars
> And linerboard to cherish.

> Chorus: You're too stund to follow me,
> Weep now in yer hanky,
> I am off to Florida
> And leave you home with Frankie.

Comparing the quality of the Smallwood roast unfa-
vourably with an earlier roast of Robert Stanfield, the *Globe*

and Mail added that the show was saved by the performance of Canon Earle from whom the Canadian public would like to hear more.

Canon Earle now and then expressed awareness that some of his more pious readers and listeners might be offended by his humour and, as he put it in one talk, denounce him as a "loose Canon." But aside from 'Mary Phool' and her friends, who castigated him on an openline radio show, only one person criticized him to his face, a woman in a Notre Dame Bay community who accosted him, "Sir, you are a discredit to the cloth." Far from being apologetic, Canon Earle publicly pled for more humour in the church. In a talk titled "Laughter in Life" he observed, "I have always thought of laughter as a tonic...and the humorous approach to life by no means indicating superficiality or lack of concern but a most faithful ally in life's most serious and solemn ventures." In his article "Humour Within the Church" he notes that in the church, as in other organizations, there is always a certain amount of "pride, vainglory, hypocrisy and not a little uncharitableness," and cites with approval Sir John Betjeman's observation that, "A sense of humour [in the Church] is a sense of proportion." If church life, Earle concluded, is to be lived at its richest, humour "cannot be confined to what is called secular but must permeate the sacred."

Earle's store of pointed anecdotes about the church and its clergy seemed to be almost inexhaustible. In a talk to the Star of the Sea Association in Holyrood in 1976 on what is now known as politically correct language he told of a Catholic nun's reaction to the ecumenism sweeping her Church, "If this keeps up I suppose we'll have to refer to Satan as a separated brother." In this, Earle assured the Association, "Protestants have already beaten you to it." He told other audiences about a man who in response to a question about the population of his community replied,

"Two hundred and sixty people and one Roman Catholic."
He reminded one audience of pre-war days in St. John's
when "the definition of an atheist was a fellow who could
watch a hockey match between St. Bon's and Feild colleges
and not care who won." Another story for religious audiences was about a Dubliner undergoing questioning at the
Northern Ireland border. Asked whether he was Protestant or Catholic, he thought he would expedite his entry by
declaring himself an atheist, but the guard shot back, "Are
you a Protestant or Catholic atheist?" George sometimes
told religious audiences about the ronk old Anglican who,
facing the fate of being buried in the community's only
cemetery, objected, "Oh my, I'd rather die than be buried
in a Methodist cemetery."

Canon Earle enjoyed poking fun at bishops and lesser
clergymen. A curate invited to address Sunday school
children began, "I want to speak to every child in the hall,
be he a boy or be he a girl, but I am sorry to see before me
many absent faces with which I have been accustomed to
shake hands." Of a canon's didactic prayer a worshipper
quipped, "That was the finest prayer ever given to a Bos-
ton audience." An earnest but somewhat discouraged rector prayed, "If there is a spark of holiness here, Lord, water
that spark." To illustrate the impact a clergyman can have
on the morals and language of a village George told about
the day the rector was taking afternoon tea with his host-
ess on her beautiful lawn when out rushed her young son
holding a dead rat. To his mother's hysterical reaction, the
boy soothed, "Don't be afraid mother — he's dead. We
beat him and bashed him until" — catching sight of the
rector — "God called him home."

Canon Earle was usually able to relate his own vocation as a clergyman to the work of his audiences. Thus to a
convention of bakers he began, "We have this in common
that we both must leaven lumps — the only difference is

that I don't have your dough;" and to the Atlantic Association of Fruit and Vegetable Growers, "Whereas you expect
a hundred percent return on the seeds you scatter, clergymen expect only twenty-five percent. But in both cases we
know the rewards by their fruits." In addressing a banquet
of engineers after a prolonged cocktail hour, the Canon
began, "It might seem strange to find a clergyman addressing a crowd of engineers after a generous and continuous
reception, but my Master was accused of being a winebib-
ber and a friend of publicans and sinners, so I am pleased
to be in your company." This talk was one of Earle's
funniest. But characteristically the message is serious. "We
must break down barriers between priest and scientist and
engineer, and see the interdependence of all hu-
mans...that man may develop culturally and spiritually as
well as materially." As for the propriety of clergymen
celebrating with engineers and winebibbers Earle concluded, "Laughter and joy do not mean superficiality or
insincerity in the Christian — a long face is not an indica-
tion of inward holiness."

The Retirement Years

In an interview with the MUN *Gazette* (June 15, 1979) on the eve of his retirement from Queen's College Canon Earle was asked about his plans for the future. He was keenly looking forward, he replied, to gardening, travel in Canada and Europe, writing a book to preserve "the endless notes I've made on things around Newfoundland," catching up on more scholarly reading and serving the Church as opportunities arose. "I've never been bored in my life....An old horse goes out to pasture and doesn't work but just eats and eventually dies. I don't do that. I'm just going to do something else." As it turned out, he did all of the things he mentioned, while continuing his after-dinner speaking and lecturing and even taking up acting as Jethro Noddy in the CBC's television series *Yarns from Pigeon Inlet*. Earle's retirement years, until he was stricken with several illnesses and more or less confined to his home, were stimulating and productive.

Canon Earle's first speech after his retirement was his address to a Memorial University convocation, spring 1979, when he was awarded a doctor of laws degree after being cited by George Story in a parody of "Wadham's Song:"

> George Halden Earle, wit, scholar; yet
> Theologian, preacher, poet,
> Whom now with warm and hearty 'plause

For the Degree of Doctor of Laws,
I present to you, our friend and brother:
Confer degree, Sir, and watch my bobber.

Of the honour, Earle remarked, "For this, to me, is the summit — to be honoured in this way by the University from which I graduated forty-six years ago," when there were a handful of faculty members and just over a hundred and fifty students. The address reviewed his experience in coming from Fogo to Memorial College, stressed the importance of "old foolishness" and, while lauding higher education, reminded the students of the old fisherman who observed, "We got no education but we uses our heads." Among the scores of groups addressed in the next decade were the Wessex Society of Newfoundland, Burin Peninsula Senior Citizens, a library association in Yarmouth, The Mining Association of Nova Scotia, a Point Leamington school graduation, the Canadian Association of Law Libraries and a seminar on teacher evaluation.

In 1987 Earle edited a collection of his speeches first titled *Firkin Around in Newfoundland*, but published as *Old Foolishness or Folklore?* (Harry Cuff Publications). The doggerel chosen to illustrate or supplement the text includes "Kip Stiddy Parson," "The Yankee and the Newf," "Our B'y Joey," "Henry Jarge's Giant Squid" and the more widely known "Come Home to Old Newfy." The copy of *Old Foolishness* George gave me is inscribed, "To a friend — saint or sleeveen but not C of E — whose books I have enjoyed as much as I hope he will enjoy this." The book, with some new material, was reprinted as *A Collection of Foolishness & Folklore* in 1988. Two of the essays, "Humour Within the Church" and "How We Got Around Then," had appeared, with selections from Jessie Mifflen, Cyril Poole, Ted Russell and Otto Tucker, in *A Yaffle of Yarns* (Harry Cuff Publications, 1985).

In 1988 and 1989 Earle wrote for the *Newfoundland Herald* a series of over forty short articles on Newfoundland words, i.e. words that had remained in use here after they had disappeared from the language of their places of origin or had taken on a new meaning in Newfoundland — roughly the definition of a Newfoundland word adopted by the *Dictionary of Newfoundland English*. The long list includes such everyday words as brewis, clean (completely), dwall or dwoll, firk, flankers, killick, liveyer, nish, pook, room (fishing station) and yaffle. Examples of usage are generally taken from George's Change Islands background. He had encountered two of our best known words, brewis and gaffer, albeit with different meanings, in the north of England. There brewis is a dish of sliced bread soaked in fat broth, having earlier denoted a dish of bread boiled in fat with salt meat and vegetables. The Newfoundland dish substituted fish for meat. Gaffer, on the other hand, bears no such resemblance to its original meaning. First used as a term of respect or seniority prefixed to a title, for example a gaffer manager, even the archbishop was referred to as the Gaffer Bishop. In the coal mining district of North England Vicar Earle was sometimes referred to as "the church gaffer." Later relegated to dialect, the term was generally used of an old man, especially a respected rustic. In Newfoundland the relation between gaffer and its original meaning became further obfuscated when it was adapted to denote a young boy, especially an assistant or apprentice to older men.

When George was writing on Newfoundland words he was also preparing for publication three lengthy excerpts from his 1938 *Argonaut* diary, and these appeared in the *Newfoundland Quarterly* between Winter 1989 and Autumn 1990. Often looking back with nostalgia, he knew that old ways, like the old language, had gone into history. As he observed in the introduction to the excerpts, "I feel it worthwhile to pass on some of this before I pass on myself because the area we covered [in the *Argonaut*] has changed so much over fifty years since then — changes in lifestyle, means of communication, standard of living and outlook, to mention but a few." The *Argonaut* diary is one of the richest primary documents on outport life in the pre-war years. Along with his Newfoundland writing, in his retirement years Canon Earle wrote some sermons as a guest preacher here and there, and several speeches on miscellaneous topics.

George and Elna were now also able to indulge their interest in travel. The first major trip was made in September 1979, when they flew to Calgary, drove through the Rockies with friends and took a 24-hour bus ride to southern California. After visiting a girlhood friend of Elna's in Vancouver, they returned to the Maritimes by train and, following visits to Halifax and Yarmouth, arrived home after a two-month absence. But England remained their chief attraction, Elna Northumberland born and George the ardent Anglophile who had staged the patriotic school concert in Seldom to mark the Silver Jubilee of George V. They also visited Holland, Italy, Portugal, Spain and Bermuda. Of course they made frequent trips around the bays of Newfoundland including a few nights in Change Islands. The Earles made several major trips with George's second cousin and great friend Brian Earle and his wife Dorothy. Summers also saw George firkin around in his garden, first in Topsail and after 1984 at 5 Howlett Avenue, St. John's.

But George still found his keenest pleasure in yarning and talking old foolishness in the "twine lofts" of his friends and relatives, usually at dinner parties but sometimes, when the solemnity of the game allowed it, at the regularly scheduled bridge parties. In his "Friends," published in *Old Foolishness*, he lamented the fact that during

Topsail c.1980. "My favourite scoff, my son!"

his long years in England he had lost contact with some of his friends, but expressed pleasure in making new ones on his return, especially "funny hands" like Otto Tucker. "You write books together and exchange yarns and play practical jokes on one another and compare notes on after-dinner speeches and join the same societies and even act together on CBC television." "And I toast all my readers," the last sentence reads, "especially those whom I may be permitted and privileged to call friends." For George's friends it was always a special pleasure to be at parties with him. Even in banter with wits like Otto Tucker and Bruce Woodland, George usually took or was gladly given centre stage. As he once said of his grandfather Earle, he was always "a concert unto himself." It was to my great joy that I could often attend these twine loft soirees.

When the excuse for parties was a birthday, an honour bestowed on a friend or any other celebration George sometimes contributed in verse. Anyone being honored, especially 'Methodists,' had to be braced for backhanded compliments and even digs at their religion or place of origin. His salute to his friend Otto Tucker on his seventieth birthday recalls Tucker's boyhood in Winterton (Scilly Cove) and his early years as a Salvation Army officer.

> We salute the chap from Scilly Cove
> Who left to serve the Man Above;
> And taught and preached with Pauline zeal
> And made his flock believe and feel.
> Back home, with stearins and buck goats
> He never did get used to boats,
> So chose to fish in human seas
> And Church of England cemeteries.

For all his learning and zeal, Tucker, sadly, never joined the true religion:

> This erstwhile Envoy soon matured,
> With higher studies he endured,
> And reached the top whate'er that be —
> But never joined the C of E.

On one occasion I found myself the subject of a rhymed 'tribute' titled "Saint or Sleeveen?." Read in January, 1983 at one of the 'outport' parties for which Mose and Grace Morgan were celebrated, it saluted my becoming a grandfather for the first time.

Come meet the chap from Pilley's Isle
In whom his mum could see no guile;
But mums think thus with risk and peril
When such a chap is our Cyril.
His pious look in Church and School
Showed not the real Cyril Poole,
For he sinned oft with mind and hand
In old, religious Newfoundland.

He smoked and chewed and told big lies,
And stretched the size of fish and flies;
On school inspectors he was hard,
He'd Bible stories disregard;
He stole the girlfriends of his foes
And laughed at Hedley's cast-off clothes;
He 'looked down' from his narrow perch
On members of the English Church.

The double-edged toast ends, "He sits before us calm and cool/We toast him — Grandpa Cyril Poole." Despite its calumnies, I was delighted and flattered when this celebration of my grandfatherly status turned up three years later in the Anglican Canon's *Old Foolishness*.

Another poem, "Mary Phool of Mussel Gut," written for the private chuckle of friends, fell into the hands of the media and brought down on the author a whirlwind of abuse. The poem was occasioned by George's hearing on open-line radio an outport girl working in St. John's launching a tirade against the bay and baymen. "I come een to St. John's last year to get a job and I went back over the weekend for a holiday and they laughed at me. I got some mad and come right back and that's me last time." Recalling how in his Change Islands boyhood some natives would return from towns or cities haughty and stuck-up, George concluded that the radio caller was of that ilk.

Come hear the yarn of Mary Phool
Who left the bay on leaving school;
She scarcely knew a verb from noun
But knew enough to go to town.
And so she left the little hut
That was her home in Mussel Gut.

In town she got a job and cash
And bought herself all kinds of trash;
She scorned the lingo of the bay
And tried to walk the towny way.
She trained herself to walk and strut
Unlike the folks of Mussel Gut.

The liveyers laughed her out of the harbour.

"Don't come here showing off to us
To make us laugh or mad and cuss;
Don't think we're easy to impress
With fancy talk and fancy dress;
Act like yourself and not a mutt
When you come back to Mussel Gut."

When "Mary Phool" was read on Ron Pumphrey's open-line show the reaction, George recalled, "was swift and nasty," the poet (his identity not given) reviled for "making fun at bay girls." George's reply was a four-verse parody of the attack.

"I'd like to get me hands on he,
The hignorant son of a she;
I'd like to claw his dirty face
And shove en een his proper place."
Said Pumphrey [radio host], "Don't be sinister
The author is a minister."

"Some minister to write that stuff
About the bay girls being tough;
There's plenty worse ones in the town
Why don't you start to run them down?
I hope we never hears no more
From that old dirty hangashore."

Both "Mary Phool" and the reply were later published in *Old Foolishness*.

By the late 1980s George's activities were curtailed by severe arthritis in his knees, the first of several ailments he was to suffer. But among the handful of activities he was determined to attend were the meetings of the Wessex Society of Newfoundland. Founded in 1984 to promote knowledge and appreciation of Newfoundland's historical connection with the West Country of England, this Society had a special appeal for the Anglophile in George. Moreover, with friends and like-minded people making up the membership, the Society's emphasis was more on the experience of ordinary people, or folklore, than on textbook history. Earle himself spoke to the Society on at least two occasions. Indeed the last major speech he gave, before illness more or less confined him to his home, was a talk on Newfoundland dialect at a Wessex Society dinner in St. John's in 1993 in honour of members of the Wessex Newfoundland Society in Poole, Dorset, who were on a two-week tour of the Province. Adding to the pleasure George derived from his association with the Wessex Society was the fact that the meetings were presided over by his friend Otto Tucker. It was in recognition of Canon Earle's longtime celebration of our West Country origins that he had been elected Honorary Life President of the Wessex Society at its founding meeting on October 25, 1984.

At the founding meeting of the Society, President Tucker, a great believer in symbols and monuments, proposed that a pub-counter towel just brought from England by his friend Leslie Karagianis be adopted as the Society's emblem. This symbol inspired the thought that the Society should also have its own song or ode. And so George's "The Wessex Towel" was enthusiastically adopted on February 18, 1985.

> All kinds of animals and tools,
> All kinds of trees and flowers
> Are used by peoples of the earth
> To symbolize their powers.
> Some use the stars and some the sun,
> The cross or crescent moon,
> A hammer or a maple leaf,
> A beaver or a loon.
> We Wessex folk in Newfoundland
> Might choose a fish or fowl,
> But as of now we only have
> This beer-marked Wessex Towel.

The "Wessex Towel" was read by President Tucker at a meeting following George's death on May 10, 2000 as part of the Society's tribute to its beloved Honorary Life President.

Meanwhile it was also in his retirement years that George appeared as Jethro Noddy in the CBC television series *Yarns from Pigeon Inlet*. Producer Tom Cahill, considering him "tailor made" for the role, offered it to him without audition. "He had," said Cahill in *The Downhomer*, January 1996, "a wonderful face and a wonderful smile and twinkle in his eye, with a little bit of devilment." The devilment sometimes got in the way of George's acting. During the filming of one show Jethro and Grampa Walcott (Otto Tucker) in a solemn scene burst out laughing, and had to be rebuked by the director, Bob Petrie, "This is costing the CBC a fortune....Let's be serious."

Ted Russell's Jethro and George were no strangers, the character having been known in Change Islands. Jethro lived by his wits, a subscriber to the view that only fools and horses work. Of his portrayal of this lazy philosopher and prankster George remarked, "I'm probably having difficulty in conveying the 'lazy' idea..., but the 'twinkle' or 'mischievous' characteristics come through quite well" (*Weekender*, Nov. 1986). Even though he realized that some pious people might question the propriety of a priest's portraying such a sleeveen as Jethro, George himself found it 'natural.' "There is," he remarked, "dignity in all Ted's characters. They survived through laughter."

Already a household name in Newfoundland, Canon Earle was now instantly recognized as Jethro wherever he went. While touring Random Island in 1986 he drove to Lower Lance Cove and on stepping out on the wharf was greeted by an old man, "You're from Change Islands, eh?" "Yes, how did you know that?" "Well," replied the old codger, "I got a daughter married in Twillingate." This would have been a baffling reply to anyone but Jethro. "Now I knew," George wrote, that "that had nothing in the world to do with it, but recognized that it was one of these cases where Newfoundlanders think they know who you are, but won't say in case they are wrong." It was the reticent bayman's indirect, convoluted way of confirming what he already knew. When a moment later George asked the old fellow his name, he replied, "You don't have to tell me yours because I watches all them *Pigeon Inlets*." On another occasion on a bus George overheard an elderly man say to his wife, "That's Jethro Noddy from the *Amos 'n' Andy Show*." In this case the fan had the wrong show, but, said George, "that made no odds." (These stories are told in the essay "At Random.")

Although after his retirement from Queen's College in 1979 Canon Earle travelled widely, gave numerous addresses in Atlantic Canada and spent taxing hours in rehearsal as Jethro Noddy, he was for most of that period suffering from a succession of debilitating and painful diseases. Crippling arthritis in his knees, high blood pressure and complications from medication, and chronic bronchitis were but the most prolonged of his illnesses. By 1995 he was virtually confined to his home. Yet the twinkle never left his eye. Nor, as his wife Elna recalled, did he ever grumble or complain.

In his letters to me during his most painful years he even commented on his afflictions, "one after another," with the same humorous detachment he brought to all his observations. Thus on July 13, 1995 he wrote, "I've read your book *To Cast the Anchor* and have had gout ever since." In a long letter in October of that year he suspected that his non-Anglican friend Otto Tucker was still expecting him one day to repent and bow his knee. "But he's foolish. He knows that people with arthritis can't bow the knee to anybody."

On February 5, 1997 he wrote, "Yes boy it's not been a good year but my non-Conformist nurse Elna looked after me well. Now we're busy repairing the bits left....I'm down to 1 oz., i.e. *one* ounce of J & B a day. I've been on too many drugs to repeat the past, especially the night in Corner Brook when you saw double" (the night he told me about the cat's strange demise). He listed four doctors who were then "pokin' around lookin' for more trouble." A letter of April 16, 1997 from "The Department of Foolishness, 5 Howlett Avenue," addressed "Dear Job" and signed "Jethro," catalogs the many parts of his body under repair, including some "firkin around the prostate," and asks "Let me know if you spot any area which is neglected."

My last conversation with George took place at his home on the drizzly Sunday morning of May 23, 1999. We talked about humour, whether there is humour *per se* or only national or regional humour. Showing little interest in that abstract question, he turned again to the debt he owed to his grandfather Earle and to "the funny people, the ordinary people, of Change Islands." There was much laughter as George mentioned again some of his favourite stories, recalling especially the two penny-pinching beer drinkers on the Northern Peninsula and the outport visitor who was so thin that a local remarked of him, "Sure he's not a man at all — he's one of them x-rays off the *Christmas Seal.*" Once again he insisted that in his after-dinner talks he was "not telling stories, but illustrating the Newfoundland character."

Although there was much laughing and carrying on during that last Sunday morning visit, it was clear that, although George's spirit still sparkled, his wracked body was having serious effects on his mind. His memory span was a bit short, Elna frequently having to help him with names and events, and his speech was sometimes hesitant. When I said goodbye to him on that dark Sunday morning to return to New Brunswick it was with foreboding that I had had my last yarn with my cherished friend. His last, short letter (to Job from Jethro) November 1, 1999, ended, "My mind is fogging over so I'll stop for clarity of thought. Sorry this is not a very sensible letter — I must need a scotch." He lived for another six months. On the evening of May 9, 2000 he was able to watch with Elna a documentary on the Viking settlement in L'Anse aux Meadows, but died in his sleep the next morning.

George Earle, as Jack Harris so aptly remarked in the House of Assembly that day, was a Newfoundland treasure. In raising our old foolishness to an art and making us laugh at ourselves he enriched the lives of us all.